MYSTICAL
BRITAIN AND IRELAND

MYSTICAL

BRITAIN AND IRELAND

Richard Jones photography by John Mason

NEW HOLLAND

First published in 2005 by New Holland Publishers (UK) Ltd
London • Cape Town • Sydney • Auckland

www.newhollandpublishers.com

Garfield House, 86–88 Edgware Road, London W2 2EA, United
Kingdom

80 McKenzie Street, Cape Town 8001, South Africa

14 Aquatic Drive, Frenchs Forest, NSW 2086, Australia

218 Lake Road, Northcote, Auckland, New Zealand

10 9 8 7 6 5 4 3 2 1

ISBN 1 84330 969 6

Publishing Manager: Jo Hemmings
Senior Editor: Charlotte Judet
Cover Design and Design: Gülen Shevki-Taylor
Cartographer: William Smuts
Production: Joan Woodroffe

Reproduction by Pica Digital Pte Ltd, Singapore
Printed and bound by Kyodo Printing Co (Singapore) Pte Ltd

PAGE 1: *Corrimony cairn is an ancient burial site in Scotland.*

PAGE 2: *Glendalough 'the Glen of Two Lakes' is one of Ireland's most tranquil and mystical places.*

OPPOSITE: *The cliff-top ruins of Whitby Abbey dominate the town of Whitby and are steeped in mystery and legend.*

CONTENTS

Introduction

Long ago humankind began its ceaseless struggle with nature, to control it and to harness its energy. Ancient peoples understood little of the science of nature, but its influence was evident all around them. It was the force that caused their crops to grow, their animals to breed, their water supply to bubble from the earth, and season to follow season. In short, their very survival depended upon this mysterious force and they came to see its more physical manifestations as being gifts from their gods. Meanwhile, that which obviously controlled the overall cycle of things, the sun, came to be seen as the supreme deity, the one on which all life apparently depended and the one that primitive peoples the world over began to worship above all others.

One abiding aspect of sun-worship was the lighting of fires, since fire was believed to increase the potency of the sun. Vestiges of these ancient beliefs and rituals are still with us. For example, when we light bonfires to celebrate Guy Fawkes Night (5th November) in Britain, we are in fact following a tradition that stretches back to the Celtic festival of *Samhain* (pronounced Sow-en), which literally meant 'summer's end'. Samhain was celebrated around our 1st November, traditionally the first day of winter in the Celtic calendar. The next important festival was the winter solstice, the date when the shortening of the days – an alarming prospect for agricultural communities – came to an end and people could look forward to the longer days that would usher in the summer. From time immemorial people had seen this as a pivotal period in the cycle of the seasons, and bonfires were lit to welcome the sun back. Consequently, 25th December, and the days that surrounded it, had long been celebrated as a sacred time when, in the 4th century, Pope Julius I declared it as having been the birthday of Jesus Christ.

Around 4,000 years ago people began focusing their rituals on centres where they could come together and worship their gods. Thus it was that stone circles, such as Stonehenge, were constructed. It must be said that the original purpose of such monuments is decidedly obscure, and we will never know for certain why they were erected. But there can be little doubt that many of them were used as centres for sun worship and that they were considered as holy places. Vestiges of this sun worship would be absorbed into the practices of almost every subsequent religion. To the Romans, for example, 25th December was *Deis Natalis Invicti Solis* – the Birthday of the Unconquered Sun. Christianity, as already mentioned, chose to honour it as the birthday of Christ and, of course, the image of the risen Christ, as propagated by the early Church, borrowed a great deal from earlier deities and from the imagery of sun worship, after all was He not said to have been 'the light of the world'.

When the early Christian missionaries began their attempts to convert the native inhabitants of Britain and Ireland, it proved difficult to win them over from their deeply held beliefs, and they found them unwilling to abandon their old deities and established places of worship. The missionaries' solution was to adapt these long-held and cherished beliefs, and to either turn the Celtic deities into Christian saints or else demonize them. Meanwhile, well-established places of worship could be utilized to help in setting down the roots of the new faith. In AD 601 Pope Gregory I wrote to Abbot Mellitus, who was about to visit England, to advise him on the course of action to be taken to draw the natives away from Paganism:

'When (by God's help) you come to our most revered brother, Bishop Augustine... tell him how earnestly I have been pondering over the affairs of the English: I have come to the conclusion that the temples of the idols in England

ABOVE: *Glastonbury Abbey is probably one of the world's best-known mystical sites.*

OPPOSITE: *Thor's Cave – an awe-inspiring and impressive sight in rural Staffordshire.*

should not on any account be destroyed. Augustine must smash the idols, but the temples themselves should be sprinkled with holy water and altars set up in them in which relics are to be enclosed. For we ought to take advantage of well-built temples by purifying them from devil worship and dedicating them to the service of the true God. In this way, I hope the people (seeing their temples are not destroyed) will leave their idolatry and yet continue to frequent the places as formerly, so coming to know and revere the true God.'

So it was that Christian churches were sited at places that had been considered holy since time immemorial, and no doubt much of their power was derived from the spiritual atmosphere that was associated with the site on which they stood.

In essence, that is the subject of this book, which lists over a hundred such sites that have long been considered mystical. Obviously, places such as Stonehenge, Avebury, Tara and Newgrange loom large, but you will also find details of lesser known sites which, to me at least, had a far more mystical feel to them, simply because they are so little known that few visitors chance upon them. I have tried

to reach a balance between pre-Christian and Christian sites, and this has necessitated omitting several well-known foundations and attractions, particularly in those places where there tended to be clusters of cathedrals, churches, monastic sites, standing stones or other prehistoric attractions. It is, of course, inevitable that a book such as this becomes a very personal collection, especially given the subject matter involved. But I honestly believe that everyone will find something of interest in its pages, whether you are seeking an ancient chapel to visit or an even older stone circle in which to ponder the mysteries of life.

One thing that was noticeable to both myself and the book's photographer, John Mason, as we visited some of the sites, was how so many people are now gravitating towards older places of worship. We were both surprised when, particularly in Ireland, we arrived at ancient monuments to find people either meditating amongst the stones, or else actually leaning against them attempting to absorb their earth energies. Herein lies one of the paradoxes of our age. For whereas meditating is an invigorating and restorative practice, the modern new age habit of lying against the stones, with feet or backs resting on them, trying to *connect* with their earth energies, almost borders on vandalism and a great deal of damage is being done to many ancient monuments by certain *nouveau* pagans who indulge in such irresponsible practices as lighting candles, or even worse, fires, around the stones – the heat from which does untold damage to the ancient and delicate fabrics. I know that the majority of more responsible and respectful visitors to these wonderful old places will agree with my criticism.

The problem for many of us today is that we live in an age that knows the price of all things and the value of nothing. Old certainties have been eaten away by the advances of science and technology. Organized religion is failing us, as demonstrated by the rapid decline in church attendance rates. Ancient people (the exquisite monuments they have left behind preclude me from referring to them by their more common description of 'primitive') would no doubt have given their right arms to enjoy the benefits of our modern age, but those benefits have been acquired at a price. Many of us are searching for *something* in this throwaway age of instant celebrity. Humankind by its very nature needs something, or someone, to believe in, and at these places where our distant ancestors found the elusive means of communion with whatever gods they worshipped or turned to in times of need, we can find it. When we have spent a few moments of quiet contemplation at these places, we come away spiritually recharged and more understanding of the enchantment that is still to be found at so many sites that lie scattered around mystical Britain and Ireland.

Richard Jones
November 2004
www.haunted-britain.com

The Realm of Dream and Mystery

✴

AND GOD STANDS WINDING HIS LONELY HORN,
AND TIME AND THE WORLD ARE EVER IN FLIGHT;
AND LOVE IS LESS KIND THAN THE GREY TWILIGHT,
AND HOPE IS LESS DEAR THAN THE DEW OF THE MORN.

FROM 'INTO THE TWILIGHT'
BY W. B. YEATS (1865–1939)

CORNWALL & SOMERSET

Cornwall exerts a powerful and magical spell over those who roam its lanes and byways in search of its secret and sacred places. '…[It] is pre-eminently the region of dream and mystery'. wrote Thomas Hardy in 1870, describing his first experience of Cornwall. Few who have stood on its windswept cliffs or gazed upon the mysterious standing stones that dot the landscape can disagree with his description. It is an otherworldly gateway to a mystical realm, across which the spirit of that most legendary of kings, Arthur, strides like a colossus. Further north and you come to the bleak desolation of Devon's Dartmoor, which has a distinctly different aura about it, part fearsome, part tranquil. Pride of place in this most spiritual of regions must go to Somerset and its fabled Isle of Avalon where the Holy Grail may lie buried and Christ himself my have walked in ancient times.

PREVIOUS PAGES: *Glastonbury Tor – one of the world's best known mystical sites. Is Glastonbury Abbey the burial place of King Arthur?*

MEN-AN-TOL
NR. MORVAH, CORNWALL
The Stone of The Hole

This enigmatic monument sits mysteriously on gorse-carpeted moorland. It consists of two standing stones, together with a rough, round middle stone, the centre of which is pierced by a hole approximately 45cm (18in) in diameter. It is from this that the monument gets its name *Men-an-Tol*, meaning simply 'stone of the hole'. No one is really certain of the exact age of this curious stone, although there is general consensus that it dates from the Bronze Age, approximately 3,000 to 4,000 years ago. Its original purpose is even more difficult to pinpoint and theories range from its having been an astronomical observatory for estimating the rising and setting of either solar or lunar events; a chambered tomb of which just the holed stone or entrance now remains; or even a stone circle from which only this ragged handful of stones has survived. William Borlase (1695–1772), the antiquarian, was convinced that the holed stone was used by the 'Cornish Druids' to '…initiate, and dedicate Children to

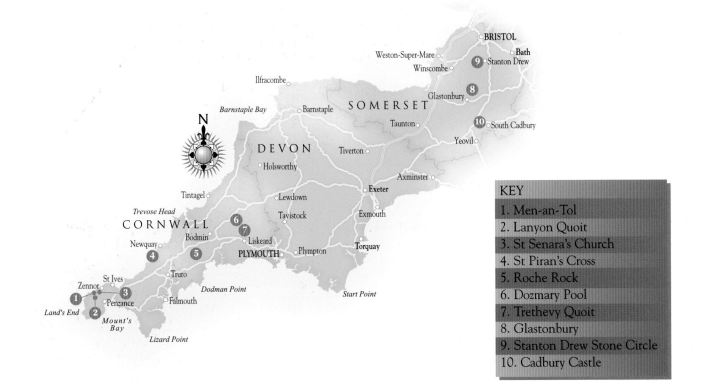

KEY
1. Men-an-Tol
2. Lanyon Quoit
3. St Senara's Church
4. St Piran's Cross
5. Roche Rock
6. Dozmary Pool
7. Trethevy Quoit
8. Glastonbury
9. Stanton Drew Stone Circle
10. Cadbury Castle

the Offices of Rock-Worship, by drawing them through this hole, and also to purify the Victim before it was sacrificed.'

Folklore and legend amply compensate for the lack of hard historical facts by giving the stones certain curative properties. It has long been held that the stones, particularly the holed middle stone, are imbued with the power to cure certain ailments in young and old alike. When William Borlase visited the site in 1749 a 'very intelligent farmer of the neighbourhood' told him about the 'many persons who had crept through this holed Stone for pains in their back and limbs'. It was because of this usage that the middle stone also became known as 'the Crickstone', since people would crawl through it in the belief that it would act as a remedy for a crick in the back. The farmer also told how 'fanciful parents at certain times of the year, do customarily draw their young children through in order to cure them of Rickets.'

The holed stone also appears to have possessed the ability to act as an oracle. There was a local belief that if two brass pins were laid across each other and left on the top edge of the middle stone, they would be given a curious predictive mobility whereby they could answer any questions put to them. Answers would be discerned by how much and in which direction the pins had actually moved when the questioner returned to the site.

Men-an-Tol is a weathered remnant of a distant past that still manages to retain its secrets. Come to it in the early silence of a winter's day, when a carpet of crisp frost surrounds it, and you can truly feel the spirit of the place as the magic of the stones draws you closer to the mysterious and forgotten people who long ago left their enigmatic mark on this Cornish moor.

RIGHT TOP: *There was a time when Cornwall's Men-an-Tol was considered to be imbued with curative properties.*

RIGHT BELOW: *Although Lanyon Quoit is now but a shadow of its former glory, an air of grandeur still pervades around it.*

LANYON QUOIT
NR. MADRON, CORNWALL
A Horseman Rode Through

This huge and impressive dolmen is now little more than a shadow of its former self. Indeed, there are accounts from the 18th century claiming that it was then possible to pass beneath the giant capstone on horseback. In 1815 the combined effects of time and the elements proved too much for the ancient monument, and in the course of a fearsome storm it gave up its defiant stance and collapsed onto the earth.

The locals, however, were not about to let such a remarkable landmark lie forgotten. They launched a

campaign for the necessary funds, and in 1824 they set about restoring it to its former glory. Unfortunately, in the course of this restoration they managed to break one of the upright supports, and thus it is that the three surviving uprights had to be shortened and squared off before the mighty capstone could be replaced on top of them. If this indignity was not sufficient to dent the pride of the ancient survivor, the quoit was also rotated by ninety degrees with the consequence that it now stands at right angles to its original position. But even after all this, Lanyon Quoit still manages to retain its majesty and there can be little doubt that, reduced as it is in size, it is still an imposing and awe-inspiring sight.

The capstone is simply huge and measures 5.3 by 2.7m (17 by 9ft), while its weight has been estimated at a remarkable 13.5 tons. As to its original purpose, it is believed to be the remains of a long barrow or chambered tomb that, it has been estimated, dates from around 2500 BC. Faint traces of the barrow can still be seen stretching for 8m (27ft) on a roughly south-north axis. There is a local legend that the bones of a giant were discovered inside the tomb, and this has led to the quoit also being known as 'The Giant's Table' or 'The Giant's Tomb'. Not one to be omitted from the folklore that surrounds such an impressive and inspiring landmark, Arthur is attached to the site, for tradition maintains that it was here that he enjoyed his last meal before the battle of Camlann.

ST SENARA'S CHURCH
ZENNOR, CORNWALL
The Mermaid of Zennor

The delightful church of St Senara, situated in the lovely seaside village of Zennor, cowers in a hollow under the granite mass of Zennor Hill. Although the earliest records we have of the present beautiful building date from 1150, it is certain that a church of some sort has stood on this site since at least the 6th century, when Irish and Breton missionaries came to Cornwall.

Tucked away in a side aisle of the church is a time-worn wooden chair on which can clearly be seen the scars that 500 plus years of constant usage have inevitably left upon its surface. On the chair's side there is a curious carving of a mermaid, a symbol which had several interpretations for medieval worshippers. Before the Christian era, mermaids were one of the symbols of Aphrodite, goddess of the sea and love. In one hand she held a quince (love apple) and in the other a comb. Later the quince was changed to a mirror, symbol of vanity and heartlessness. She was seen by medieval Christians as a symbol of lust, and a warning against the sins of the flesh. But she also had another more inspirational interpretation amongst seafaring communities where she was also used to illustrate the two natures of Christ. As she was both human and fish-like, so Christ could be both human

and divine, a message that would have struck a chord with the inhabitants of this isolated region whose lives were both dependent upon and intertwined with the sea.

However, later ages were to imbue this little chair with a fanciful legend that has an eerie supernatural quality. Many years ago, so the story goes, the people of Zennor were curious about a mysterious, though finely dressed lady who each Sunday attended the evening service at their church. She would sit at the back of the church listening to the choir. She was especially fond of the singing of a boy named Matthew Trewhella, and it wasn't long before she had fallen in love with him. The woman, it transpired, was a mermaid who had been lured from the sea by the sweet sound of Matthew's voice, and one Sunday she could contain her feelings no longer. Casting a spell over him, she lured him from the church, led him along the tiny stream that still babbles through the centre of the village today, and finally took him with her back into the sea. Matthew Trewhella was never seen again, but one Sunday morning, many years later, some sailors on a ship anchored in a nearby cove claimed that they were surprised by a mermaid who rose from the water and asked the captain to raise his anchor, because it was barring the entrance to her home. They recognized her instantly as the enigmatic woman who had visited the church, and thus the tale spread of how Matthew Trewhella had been taken from them by this lovely creature of the sea to become her

lover. Locals claimed that on warm summer evenings they could often hear the voices of the two lovers carried on the sea breezes, singing in perfect harmony together.

ST PIRAN'S CROSS
PENHALE SANDS, CORNWALL
He Came Back From the Depths

Almost lost amidst the dunes of Penhale Sands, this 2.5m (8ft) high cross is the oldest recorded stone cross in Cornwall. It was mentioned in a charter of King Edgar in AD 960, by which time it was already an old landmark. The cross commemorates one of the county's patron saints, St Piran, or Perran. Although his family origins are obscure, it is generally believed that he came to Cornwall from Ireland when some of the native Irish became jealous of his healing powers and of his ability to work miracles. During an horrendous thunderstorm they tied a millstone around his neck and threw him from a cliff into the sea. They had, however, underestimated his abilities, for no sooner had the saint hit the surface than the storm suddenly abated and Piran bobbed back up to the surface. Waving farewell to Ireland he set course for Cornwall, sailing on the millstone that his would-be executioners had tied around his neck. It carried him to Cornwall where he came ashore between Newquay and Perranporth, at a spot that is still known as Perran Beach in his memory. Here he settled into a life of renewed holiness and built himself a small chapel on Penhale Sands, where his first disciples are said to have been a badger, a bear and a fox.

St Piran is attributed with discovering tin in Cornwall (although it would be more accurate to say that he rediscovered what the Romans had previously discovered). The story goes that he built himself a fireplace from a large chunk of black rock. As the flames grew hotter he was amazed when a trickle of pure white metal began to ooze out of the stone. He shared the knowledge of his discovery with the indigenous population who quickly capitalized upon this natural resource and thus was begun the lucrative Cornish tin trade. As a result of his find he is also the patron saint of tin miners, and the seeping white metal, his most enduring legacy to Cornwall, features as the white cross of St Piran that is set against a black background on the Cornish flag. Inevitably, his story has become intertwined with another famous figure from Cornwall's past, King Arthur, and legend has also chosen to remember him as Arthur's personal chaplain.

St Piran is said to have been a convivial man who was famed for liking his drink, a fondness that eventually led to his demise, since he is said to have either drunk himself to death or to have fallen into a well while under the influence of

BELOW: *Standing aloof and alone on Penhale Sands, St Piran's Cross commemorates Cornwall's patron saint.*

strong ale. Either way he had managed to reach the ripe old age of 206 and, it is claimed, never lost his youthful appearance, so perhaps his lifestyle shouldn't attract too much censure! His feast day is kept on 5th March, and every year thousands of people flock to Cornwall on the nearest Sunday to this date in order join the procession to the site of St Piran's Oratory, which now lies buried beneath Penhale Sands.

Today, this 6th-century cross is the grandest relic in the vicinity where St Piran is said to have come ashore. It possesses an aura of mystery tinged with melancholy. The surrounding landscape resonates with an otherworldly feel. It is a truly enchanting experience to visit this sea-sprayed spot as the last rays of the day sink beyond the horizon, to stand and feel the salt air against your face as you listen to the rolling waves of the sea, alone with your thoughts as the mysteries of the night engulf you.

ROCHE ROCK
NR. ROCHE, CORNWALL
A Holy Man's Rocky Residence

This solitary outcrop of black granite rises sharply from the surrounding moorland, its jagged outline able to elicit gasps of awestruck wonder from many a traveller who passes it on the roads below. There used to be a tradition that the crag had once

BELOW: *Time may have toppled much of the temporal bulk of Roche Rock's St Michael's Chapel but an aura of spirituality still emanates from its battered remains.*

been covered by earth, but during Noah's flood the layer of soil over it was washed away, leaving behind this saw-toothed chunk of splintered rock, which by the Middle Ages had gained a fearsome reputation as a convenient resting place for passing witches and demons. Perhaps that is why a succession of holy men came to the rock when Christianity was first brought to Cornwall, and lived as hermits in a small oratory that had been built between the rock's two peaks. Their prayers served to vanquish whatever evil forces were loose amidst the fearsome pinnacles, and the local people could feel safe from demonic interference and influences in their daily lives.

One such holy man is said to have been the hermit Ogrin who reputedly sheltered the lovers Tristan and Iseult in the oratory when they had incurred the wrath of Tristan's uncle, and Iseult's husband, King Mark, by falling in love and eloping together. The medieval poet Beroul, who was responsible for one of the earliest versions of the story, shows himself to have been familiar with the Cornish landscape, and his description of Ogrin's chapel certainly has more than a passing resemblance to Roche Rock.

In the 15th century a more elaborate chapel was built over the hermit's cell. It was dedicated to St Michael, the Archangel who was celebrated as a guardian of high places and subjugator of evil forces. The ruins of this chapel now loom against the skyline, and give the distinct impression of having sprouted from the granite. It is a strange and haunting place where you can begin to understand the fears and anxieties that beset those residents of long ago to whom the rock came to represent nothing less than the clash of good against evil. Only this tiny chapel, its solid walls braced against the savage onslaughts of the elements, stood as a silent though effective guardian, its benign spell offering some semblance of protection against the malevolent forces that, it was believed, were everywhere. After a few moments of contemplative solitude you can feel a closeness to those holy men who forsook their worldly comforts and dedicated themselves to a life of mystical loneliness, sustained only by their prayers and faith.

DOZMARY POOL

NR. BOLVENTOR, CORNWALL

The Rippling Waters Where Excalibur May Lie

There is a strange and awesome desolation about the wilderness of Bodmin Moor. To walk across its bleak expanse is to feel that you have strayed into a nether region, a timeless limbo where the souls of previous ages hover precariously close to the present. Celtic crosses lean wearily against the unforgiving terrain. Mysterious stone circles huddle together, jealously guarding their ancient secrets. Long-abandoned mine buildings stand gaunt against the skyline, their dark silhouettes often enveloped in thick mists that lend them a ghostly air. At the heart of the moor is Dozmary Pool, a grim expanse of still, leaden water surrounded by low, brown, treeless hills where a legion of legends come marching from a mist-shrouded past.

It was to the rock-strewn edges of this melancholic pool that Sir Bedivere is said to have brought the dying King Arthur, who instructed him to cast Excalibur into its sullen waters. It doesn't take a great leap of the imagination to picture Bedivere trudging down to the reed-fringed banks where he found himself unable to dispose of so beautiful a sword. Twice he returned to his dying King who knew from the answers to his questions that his wish had not been carried out. On the third occasion, however, the loyal knight had reluctantly complied with Arthur's wishes, and thus when questioned was, according to Tennyson, able to reply:

… With both hands I flung him, wheeling him;
But when I looked again, behold an arm,
Clothed in white samite, mystic, wonderful,
That caught him by the hilt, and brandish'd him
Three times, and drew him under in the mere'.

Arthurian epics aside, the pool has several other legends to fire the imagination of even the most jaded city dweller. At night a dark spirit is said to sit by the lifeless waters, its despairing cries clearly discernible over even the wildest of autumn gales. He is known locally as Jan Tregeagle and his dreadful spectre has, it is whispered, been doomed to eternal torment for the dreadful atrocities he committed in life.

Jan Tregeagle lived in the early 1600s and was a none too popular local magistrate said to have used his position to make himself very wealthy. Local tradition holds that he murdered his wife and children, seized an orphan's estates and even sold his soul to the Devil. That an unsympathetic and unpopular magistrate named Tregeagle existed is historic fact. Whether he ever sold his soul to the Devil, murdered his wife and children or seized the estates of orphans to swell his own coffers, as is claimed, is doubtful. But such was the low esteem in which he was held that it was said that he had

ABOVE: *The desolate waters of Dozmary Pool into which Sir Bedivere is said to have thrown Arthur's sword.*

to bribe the clergy to ensure that his body would be buried in the consecrated ground of St Breock's churchyard.

A few years after his death, a land dispute arose between two Bodmin families, one of which had once employed Jan Tregeagle as their lawyer, and had subsequently been defrauded by him when he forged certain documents to make it appear that he was the legal owner of the disputed lands. When both sides had presented their cases and the judge was ready to sum up, the defendant asked if he could call one final witness. Suddenly the air turned cold, a blast of wind howled through the courtroom, and the spirit of Jan Tregeagle appeared in the witness box. He was forced, under oath, to admit that the defendant had been a victim of his fraud. Upon hearing this the jury brought in a unanimous verdict in the man's favour. Arguing that the business of bringing Tregeagle from the grave had been an onerous and frightful task, the victorious defendant ignored the judge's command to remove the fearsome spectre from the room, and thanking the jury, left the phantom in the care of the court.

The assistance of the clergy was duly called upon and they decided that it was their moral duty to attempt to save Tregeagle's troubled soul. So they set him a task that, they hoped, would keep him busy for the rest of eternity. Thus he was brought to the boggy banks of Dozmary Pool and condemned to empty its bottomless depths with a perforated limpet shell. To ensure that he kept hard at his task, they cast spells and summoned forth a pack of demon hounds to snap at his heels should he ever falter in his impossible and endless task. Many is the late-night wanderer who has mistaken his anguished shrieks of frustrated rage for nothing more than the innocent howling of the wind!

TRETHEVY QUOIT
Nr. St Cleer, Cornwall
Arthur's Quoit

One of England's most impressive dolmens, Trethevy Quoit is known locally as 'The Giant's House', and its overall appearance has changed little since 1598 when it was described as being 'a little howse raysed of mightie stones, standing on a little hill within a fielde'. Indeed, such are the impressive dimensions of this spectacular Neolithic chamber tomb that legend has long imbued it with the spirit of the most enigmatic of Britain's folk heroes and bestowed upon it the alternative name of 'Arthur's Quoit'.

Historically speaking the dolmen dates from the Megalithic period and was originally covered by a cairn or mound. This has long since been worn down to a tiny hillock and only the upright stone supports are left, surmounted by their enormous capstone, or quoit, standing sullen and alone in the middle of a field. A haunting relic of a bygone and forgotten age that gives the overall appearance of having been left shipwrecked by time.

The inner tomb is accessed via a small aperture where food may once have been left to sustain the occupant on his or her journey into the afterlife. It has also been suggested that the narrow entrance may have been intended as a means by which the spirit of the departed could go free. At some stage in the past the support stone located at the rear of the chamber collapsed inwards and left the giant capstone tilting at the precarious angle that gives the quoit its truly dramatic appearance. Five cup-like hollows have been carved into the fallen stone, while the capstone is pierced at its highest point by a natural hole, the function of which is something of a mystery. It has been suggested that its purpose may have been astronomical, although no proof for this theory exists.

It is uncertain how the dolmen came to be associated with King Arthur. Several quoits scattered around Britain have been attributed to the legendary King, and nearly all of them have a tradition that they were thrown onto their current

LEFT: *Legend has long associated the leaning bulk of Trethevy Quoit with Britain's most enigmatic folk hero, King Arthur.*

OPPOSITE: *Glastonbury is a sacred place that has long held the mantle of the occult capital of England.*

location by Arthur in the course of one conflict or another. It is possible that Trethevy Quoit may have once been associated with some deed or battle in which the great hero featured, and although the story is now forgotten, its memory lingers on in the alternative name by which this windswept monument is known.

GLASTONBURY
SOMERSET
And did Those Feet in Ancient Times?

Glastonbury is probably one of the world's best-known mystical sites. It has been a sacred place for over 2,000 years and has connections with St Patrick, King Arthur and the Celtic god of the Underworld, Gwyn ap Nudd. There is even a tradition that, as a boy, Jesus himself visited Glastonbury in the company of his uncle Joseph of Arimathea.

The town of Glastonbury huddles in a cluster of hills, the highest of which, Glastonbury Tor (meaning rocky peak or hill), rises sheer from the Somerset Levels and dominates the adjoining countryside – a striking landmark which is visible from miles around. Long ago the surrounding land was covered by water, and for centuries the Tor was an islet known as Ynis Witrin, meaning 'Isle of Glass'. Its very isolation may well have given it a decidedly otherworldly feel and hence it came to be seen as a place where strange beings resided. Consequently, many legends came to cling to its enigmatic summit, all of which shared the common thread that this soft green hill was a place where the veil between this world and another more mysterious and hidden realm was believed to be at its thinnest.

To the Celts the Tor was the entrance to the underworld and was believed to be the home of Gwyn ap Nudd, the Lord of the Underworld. He later evolved into the King of the Fairies and the Tor, so it was believed, was the place where he held his court. As such, people came to see it as a place that was to be avoided at all costs. Local people were well aware of the dangers of straying into his realm. One of them was that you might only have spent a few hours there, yet when you returned to this world you would have found that many years had passed. Another worry was that if you accepted the hospitality of the fairies and partook of their food and drink you would never be able to leave their world again.

Christianity, of course, sought to conquer these old beliefs and so one of the Tor's most famous legends tells how St Collen, a pious 6th-century monk who lived as a hermit in a cell on top of the Tor, was invited to meet with Gwyn ap Nudd. Having declined Gwyn's offer of food, Collen proceeded to douse him in holy water, whereupon Gwyn and his court vanished, and Collen found himself alone upon the cold hillside. However, St Collen's attempts to rid the hill of the baleful influence of the fairies may not have been a complete and permanent success, for on 11th September

1275 an earthquake shook the Tor and brought the newly built Church of St Michael tumbling down. Many locals were convinced that the destruction was the work of the fairies. The church was rebuilt, but it didn't last and all that now remains of it is the gaunt tower that was added in the 1360s, and which makes a truly striking landmark.

However, Glastonbury had been sacred long before St Collen arrived upon the Tor to battle the fairies. Tradition holds that, in the early days of Christianity, St Joseph of Arimathea arrived in England to preach the Gospel and brought with him the Chalice from the Last Supper, the fabled Holy Grail into which the blood and sweat of the crucified Christ had flowed. Climbing the middle one of Glastonbury's three hills and weary from his journey, he paused to rest, and drove his staff into the ground where it took root and flowered, becoming the celebrated Glastonbury Thorn, which used to blossom every Christmas, until it was cut down by a zealous Puritan in the 17th century. Today, the hill is known as 'Wearyall Hill' in commemoration of Joseph's exhaustion, and a scion of the original thorn still grows upon its summit. Having recovered his strength, Joseph is said to have built a chapel on a site near where the ragged vestiges of Glastonbury Abbey now stand. This humble little foundation of wattle and daub was later believed to have been the first Christian church

ABOVE: *The sullen stones of Stanton Drew form a circle that is twice the size of Stonehenge. The fact that the site has never been fully excavated adds greatly to its air of mystery.*

in England, and from its foundations sprang Glastonbury's reputation as one of the holiest places on earth, a place to which pilgrims once flocked in their thousands to kneel in awe and pluck a sprig from the Holy Thorn in order that it might be buried with them, thus ensuring swift passage into heaven.

As the original chapel flourished into a magnificent monastic foundation so the legends of Glastonbury grew. We hear of St Patrick returning here to become abbot after he had converted Ireland. But the strongest and most deeply held belief of all, and the one that truly helped make Glastonbury a mystical place, was that Joseph of Arimathea had buried the Holy Grail beneath the third of Glastonbury's three hills, Chalice Hill. In the tranquil gardens beneath its slopes, ice-cold water still babbles from an ornate well-head. Heavily impregnated with iron, the red-tinged liquid, which tastes clean and fresh, was long thought to be stained with the blood of Christ. Medieval pilgrims would kneel before the spring, trembling and crying with emotion. Today, people still come to this lovely little garden to enjoy a few moments contemplation and to fill containers with the water in the hope of absorbing its spiritual qualities.

Of all the legendary figures to have been associated with Glastonbury and its abbey, few can be as famous, or as elusive, as King Arthur, whose burial place the abbey was reputed to have been. In 1184, the old abbey was destroyed by fire, its library, countless treasures as well as the hallowed little church built by Joseph of Arimathea, all perished in the flames. Henry II contributed generously to the rebuilding work and by 1186 the lovely Romanesque Lady Chapel at the west end of the church had been completed. In 1190, the monks, apparently acting on information passed to them by Henry prior to his death in 1189, began making 'strenuous efforts' to find Arthur's grave. In the abbey cemetery, having dug down to a depth of 5m (16ft), they found two skeletons in the hollowed-out trunk of an oak tree. With them was a leaden cross on which was inscribed in Latin either 'Here lies Arthur, the famous King of the Isle of Avalon' or 'Here lies Arthur, king that was, king that shall be'. Arthur's bones are said to have been much larger than those of a normal man, while Guinevere's skeleton was reputedly crowned with a splendid head of golden hair. On the 19th April 1278, the two skeletons were re-interred in a black marble tomb inside the church and from then on the abbey benefited immensely from the additional pilgrim traffic that their presence generated.

Of course, whether the remains were or were not those of Arthur and his Queen now matters little. The tomb was destroyed along with much of the abbey at the Dissolution of the Monasteries (1536–1540), and a modern plaque is all that now marks its site. But what cannot be denied is that Glastonbury is a special and mystical place and no one who arrives here early on those magical mornings when a ghostly mist smothers the surrounding fields, and the domed bulk of Glastonbury Tor rises from it, an island once again, can fail to be moved by the stunning and breathtaking sight that greets them.

STANTON DREW STONE CIRCLE
STANTON DREW, SOMERSET
Sullen, Silent Guardians of Ancient Secrets
Stanton Drew hides its glories from the prying eyes of all but the most dedicated seeker after things mystical. It lies well off the beaten track, a fact that has spared it from the destructive incursions of the modern tourist industry, which have so overwhelmed Stonehenge and which threaten Avebury with a similar fate. Indeed, unlike these more famous sites, the three stone circles at Stanton Drew have not been subjected to exhaustive excavations, nor have they been overwhelmed by a plethora of theories as to how the stones came to be there, what their original purpose was, or why ancient peoples laid them out in such patterns on the landscape. They stand sullen and solitary, their secrets safe, their solitude and character ensuring that the mystery and enchantment that

hangs over them remains intact and undisturbed.

Stanton Drew is thought to date from around 3000 BC. It is twice the size of Stonehenge and, like Avebury, consists of three stone circles, as well as a group of three stones that are known as 'The Cove' and which stand in the garden of the village pub. The Great Circle (made up of 27 stones, most of which are recumbent) is 112m (367ft) across and has the distinction of being the second largest stone circle in England after the outer ring at Avebury. Although excavation at the site has been minimal, archaeologists have recently discovered evidence of a huge structure that once stood inside the Great Circle. This suggests that the megalithic remains were part of a much more complex and important site than was previously thought. There are, however, no immediate plans for further excavation of the site and consequently the historical facts remain sparse and the stones will be allowed to keep their secrets, at least for the foreseeable future.

Where history remains mute, however, folklore and legend are only too happy to step in and provide their own intriguing explanation as to the origin of the stones. Tradition holds that they are in fact the petrified remains of a wedding party that was turned to stone by the Devil! One Saturday in the distant past, so the story goes, a great wedding feast was held in the vicinity and everyone was enjoying themselves immensely. The bride, who was a little the worse for drink, encouraged the fiddler to play on, even though the Sabbath was rapidly approaching. The fiddler refused, whereupon the bride exclaimed that the dancing would continue even if she had to go to hell to find a fiddler. It was an unwise outburst, for no sooner had the words left her mouth than a tall stranger appeared in their midst and struck up a merry jig. Faster and faster the guests twirled, swirled and spun as the dance went on and on through the night, each of them unable to stop. Come the dawn they had all been turned to stone, and the fiddler, who was, of course, the Devil himself, had seized their souls and spirited them away to the fires of hell. So it is that the sullen stones are said to be the petrified bodies of the guests, while the three stones known as 'The Cove' are, it is claimed, the mortal remains of the bride, bridegroom and parson. A delightful little legend, and one that is to be found at many stone circles throughout Britain, clear evidence of the early Church's wish to either demonize the sites of older religions or else imbue them with a moral warning in an attempt to discourage the locals from seeing them as holy and sacred places.

CADBURY CASTLE
SOUTH CADBURY, SOMERSET
Was this Camelot?
A few miles from the Dorset–Somerset border, a tree-shrouded hill looms large over the patchwork landscape of hedgerows and fields, its nebulous history extending far back into the

foggy mists of time. Having undertaken the ankle-jarring climb to the heights of what was originally an Iron Age hill-fort, the exhausted wayfarer is treated to a stunning vista of breathtaking splendour. It comes as little surprise to find that this truly regal summit has long held the crown of likeliest contender for King Arthur's Camelot.

The King Arthur of popular imagination is, of course, a medieval invention and those who arrive at Cadbury Castle expecting to find a turreted fortress of soaring walls and lofty towers, are destined for disappointment. Cadbury has never boasted that sort of Norman bastion. It is the fortified hill itself that was the castle. But, if there was an historical Arthur, he is most likely to have lived in the 5th or 6th centuries, and this is just the sort of hilltop stronghold that he would have inhabited. The first known reference to Cadbury as Camelot is from the antiquarian John Leland who wrote in 1542: 'At the very south end of the church of South-Cadbyri standeth Camallate, sometime a famous town or castle…. The people can tell nothing there but that they have heard say Arthur much resorted to Camalat….' Despite claims by sceptics that Leland invented the Camelot association, and that prior to him there was no such tradition, Arthurian lore has certainly abounded round the site ever since. An ancient track that runs from the base of the hill towards Glastonbury has long been known as King Arthur's Hunting Track. Another established tradition maintains that Arthur sleeps beyond a pair of hidden iron gates in a cave that lies deep beneath the hill. Indeed, so ingrained was this legend by the 19th century that when a group of Victorian archaeologists came to the district, an old man enquired earnestly if they had come to 'dig up the king'? As early as 1586, the highest section of the summit was known as Arthur's Palace, while on Midsummer's Night or Christmas Eve, Arthur and his Knights are said to come galloping down from the brow of the hill to water their horses in a spring beside Sutton Montis Church.

Interestingly, an archaeological investigation of the 18-acre (7-hectare) site in the 1960s revealed that the Iron Age hill-top fort had been refortified during the 6th century – the time when Arthur is believed to have flourished. So colossal was the undertaking that whoever ordered it must have been a powerful and significant figure. Of course, it is little more than romantic speculation to suggest that that figure was King Arthur. Indeed, the closest we can ever come to claiming Cadbury Castle as the site where Britain's most legendary monarch constructed his famous castle is to say cautiously 'it might have been'. Indeed, in all honesty, that is all we can say about the 'Arthurian Age'.

LEFT: *Standing on the windswept heights of Cadbury Castle it is easy to picture the age of Arthur, whose fabled Camelot this is said to have been.*

An Ancient Kingdom and Temples to Forgotten Gods

✴

Here oft, when Evening sheds her twilight ray,
And gilds with fainter beam departing day,
With breathless gaze, and cheek with terror pale,
The lingering Shepherd startles at the tale,
How, at deep midnight, by the moon's
chill glance,
Unearthly forms prolong the viewless dance;
While on each whisp'ring breeze that murmurs by,
His busied fancy hears the hollow sigh.

FROM 'STONEHENGE'
BY THOMAS STOKES SALMON (1823)

26

DORSET & WILTSHIRE

Once forming the core of the Saxon kingdom of Wessex, and dominated by the vast chalk landscape of Salisbury Plain, this tranquil land, from its mysterious hillsides to its ancient towns, is marked by history and legend. It was here under the inspired leadership of Alfred the Great that the English nation was born. Along its dusty byways, later to be littered with memories of Arthurian battles, the Roman legions marched, pausing to revive themselves in the hot natural waters at Aqua Sulis (Bath). But long before any of this, a forgotten and mysterious people had cast their shadow across the landscape. They carved strange figures onto the chalk hillsides, and erected massive earthworks, which later generations would come to believe could only have been erected by the Devil. Most impressive of all, were the two immense stone temples that they built at Avebury and Stonehenge, and which still amaze and confound us today, some 3,000 to 4,000 years later.

TRENT BARROW
NR. SHERBORNE, DORSET
The Threshold of Another Realm
This earthwork might not be the easiest place to get to, but once you have managed to manoeuvre into what little parking space is available, and trudged along the muddy track that leads to it, you genuinely feel that you have

PAGE 26: *The tomb at West Kennet is the largest long barrow in England.*

PREVIOUS PAGE: *Avebury Stone Circle, one of Britain's most impressive stone circles, is blessed with an aura that is at times fearsome but mostly tranquil.*

OPPOSITE: *The Cerne Abbas Giant is a truly striking hill figure whose greatest asset can only be truly appreciated from the air!*

KEY
1. Trent Barrow
2. Cerne Abbas
3. Badbury Rings
4. Knowlton Church
5. Stonehenge
6. White Horse
7. Avebury Stone Circles
8. Silbury Hill
9. West Kennet Long Barrow

arrived on a threshold that might admit you in to who knows what. As you stand on top of the horseshoe-shaped earthwork and gaze down into the pool below, an eerie, almost surreal, atmosphere holds sway over your senses. The banks that fall away to the shimmering water seem impossibly steep, but having struggled, or most likely slipped, down them you gaze into the mysterious depths, and waves of fear and fascination wash over you in equal measure. The pool is thought to have been one of the places into which Sir Bedivere threw Excalibur, the fabled sword of King Arthur (see page 19), and when the rays of the sun glance off the gleaming surface, you really can feel as if a portal to another world, or even another time, is about to open before you, and reality deserts you for a few short moments.

THE CERNE ABBAS GIANT
CERNE ABBAS, DORSET
A Monument to Masculine Splendour
Standing an impressive 55m (180ft) tall, the club-wielding Cerne Abbas Giant is the most detailed of all Britain's hill-figures, resplendent with eyes, nose, mouth, breasts, ribs and awesomely proportioned genitalia. It can only be truly appreciated from the air. Indeed, such is his proud and unabashed stance that he has long been regarded as a fertility symbol whose assistance has been eagerly sought by courting and married couples, many of whom, it is rumoured, have consummated their relationships between his massive chalk thighs.

The Giant's origins, however, are lost in a swirling haze of folklore and speculation. Several historians believe that he depicts the Greek god Hercules and that he was carved during the reign of the Emperor Commodus (AD 180–193) who, believing himself to be a reincarnation of Hercules, revived his cult. Legend, on the other hand, asserts that the figure represents an invading giant who fell asleep on the hillside and was decapitated by the local people, who carved his outline into the chalk as a warning to other marauders. A third hypothesis points to the fact that his 9-m (30-ft) phallus is directly aligned to the rising sun on 1st May and this, coupled with the fact that May Day celebrations were once held atop the hill above the giant's head, seems to suggest that he may have been linked to an ancient fertility ritual.

Whatever his origins, his presence has long been a source of amusement and controversy. Perhaps the last word should go to a local dignitary, the Hon. Ophelia Pashley-Cumming, who once observed: 'I have never felt affronted by the Cerne Giant, and have no time for the simpering old ladies who cluck-cluck every time they pass it. The only residents I sympathize with are the elderly males or tired Dorchester businessmen who are constantly reminded by their wives and mistresses *en passant* of how far short they fall of the splendid male vigour displayed before them..'

LEFT: *Badbury Rings is an Iron Age Hill fort where legend holds that King Arthur won one of his greatest battles over the Saxons.*

cover for the defenders. However, it gave little protection against the might of Rome, and became one of 20 similar hill-forts that fell to the legions commanded by Vespasian (a future emperor; AD 69–79) as he swept westwards towards Exeter. It is rumoured that the Romans established a town called Vindocladia just outside the fort, but since the site has never been excavated there is no archaeological evidence to back this up.

It is traditionally claimed that Badbury Rings is the location of Mons Badonicus (Mount Badon) where, in the late 5th or early 6th century, King Arthur fought his greatest battle against the Saxons. The claim is based solely on the similarity between the names Badbury and Badon and no historical evidence actually exists to suggest that this was the site, nor for that matter that such a battle ever took place! According to legend, the Saxons had promised to return to their homeland following their defeat in the north of the country. However, they instead sailed south round the coast, landed at Torbay and terrorized their way inland until they arrived at Mount Badon on the summit of which they took up an advantageous position. Furious at the broken pledge, Arthur hurried south and, raising Excalibur, threw himself up Badon's slopes, slaying 470 Saxons as he went. Emboldened by his example, his followers stormed after him, and the enemy was routed once and for all. So complete was Arthur's victory that it brought about a period of peace that would last for 21 years, until he was forced to defend his kingdom against his treacherous nephew Mordred. Furthermore, since the defeated Saxons now became settlers, rather than invaders, and began intermarrying with the native Britons, it sowed the seeds from which grew the English nation.

Given the violence of its past, legendary or otherwise, genuine feelings of peace and tranquillity pervade the air around Badbury Rings today. In summer its slopes are carpeted by red deadnettle, eyebright, buttercups, thistles

BADBURY RINGS
Nr. Wimborne, Dorset
They Resisted the Romans and Died for Their Pains

This Iron Age hill-fort was probably constructed by the Durotriges tribe, who provided the first real resistance that the Romans encountered when they commenced their invasion of Britain in AD 43. It consists of three concentric ditches that were dug to a depth of around 6m (20ft) and the resultant rubble then utilized to create a high earth rampart on the inner side of each ditch. The ramparts were probably crowned by a timber enclosure that would have provided and silverweed. Butterflies and dragonflies hover around the beech and oak trees that stand proudly upon a site that is imbued with history and mystery, a place where the tribesmen who fought bravely against the oppressive might of Rome may still lie buried.

KNOWLTON CHURCH AND EARTHWORKS
Nr. Cranborne, Dorset
A Venerated and Sacred Site?

The ruins of Knowlton Church sit peacefully at the centre of a pagan earth circle and stand as a unique testimony to a clash of religious beliefs. There are actually four enclosures at the site, of which the most impressive is the Centre Circle, which, probably out of respect for the melancholic church ruin that stands at its centre, has escaped the effects that centuries of farming have inflicted upon its near neighbours. The structure dates from between the 12th and 15th centuries and serves as an excellent example of how the Christian Church strove to plant itself in the minds and hearts of the local populace by adapting and assimilating older pagan sites and customs. It is also probable that if any standing stones were located at a site that was evidently venerated and sacred, they would have been broken up and used in the construction of the local church.

Although the site today is somewhat lonely and desolate, a thriving community once existed in the village of Knowlton. In the late 14th century the village was decimated by the Black Death. Its surviving inhabitants chose to abandon their village and migrated to Southampton and Bournemouth. Their houses gradually fell into decay and were eventually ploughed into the earth where vague traces of the foundations can still be spied a few hundred yards to the west of the church. Knowlton Church, however, remained a place of worship for several more centuries. But by the mid-1600s its congregation had fallen away and in 1659 an attempt was made to demolish it, although this was abandoned due to local opposition. Turnout appears to have revived by 1730 and it is believed that the north aisle was added around this time. But not long afterwards the roof fell in and the church's days were numbered.

Today, despite the picturesque landscape, a certain aura of melancholy hangs heavy over the site. A sacred place since ancient times, it has served as a place of worship for at least two religions, and yet for nearly 200 years has lain abandoned. Perhaps the site's essential paradox is that despite the attempts of those long-ago men of God to obliterate its pagan origins, their efforts eventually came to naught, and their church now lies in ruins, surrounded by the spirits of the older faith.

BELOW: *The ruins of Knowlton Church sit peaceably at the centre of a stone circle, as Paganism and Christianity manage to co-exist.*

STONEHENGE
Nr. Salisbury, Wiltshire
Ancient Temple to Forgotten Gods

Stonehenge exerts a powerful force that draws people from all across the globe to experience its magical aura and to stand in wonder beneath this monument to a forgotten people, whose everyday lives and beliefs can now only be guessed at. Indeed, arguments still rage over the origins of this ancient enigma, for the truth is that nobody knows for certain who it was that built it and what its original purpose was. Could it have been a place for religious rituals? Was it intended as an observatory for predicting important astronomical events? Was it used as a place of worship and sacrifice by the Druids? The truth is that we actually know very little about Stonehenge. As Lord Byron pointed out in his poem *Don Juan*: '…The Druid's groves are gone – so much the better. Stonehenge is not, but what the devil is it?'

Early mention of Stonehenge was made in 1135 by that great weaver of colourful legends, the chronicler Geoffrey of Monmouth (*c*.1100–*c*.1154). He claimed that the stones were brought from Africa to Ireland by a tribe of giants, and from there the great wizard Merlin flew them across the sea to their current location. It is worth noting that two distinctive types of stones were used in the construction of Stonehenge, bluestones and sarsens. Neither of these were readily available in the immediate vicinity. The nearest place from which stones the size of the large sarsens could have been brought from (the heaviest of which weighs in at a hefty 45 tons) is the Marlborough Downs situated 18 miles to the northeast of the site. As for the bluestones they probably came from the north flank of the Prescelly Mountains in Wales, and their transportation must have been a colossal undertaking for those times. It is believed that they were carried by raft around the coast of Wales to Bristol, then transported up local rivers and heaved overland until finally being lugged on rollers up the avenue that approaches Stonehenge. Considering the achievement of getting the stones to the site and the effort required to then erect them, is it any wonder that our more recent ancestors came to see the hand of sorcery or even the Devil in their construction?

It was the Saxons who named the stones 'Stonehenge' or the 'Hanging Stones'. In the 12th century, Henry of Huntingdon claimed that they were given this name because the stones appear to float, a claim that is made about many stone circles. However, it is also possible that the name is an over-literal translation of the Anglo Saxon *hengen*, which means both 'hanging' and 'gallows'. Medieval writers, from Geoffrey of Monmouth onwards, refer to the monument as the 'Giant's Dance' and repeat the assertion that Aurelius Ambrosius, King of the Britons, wished to construct a memorial over the burial site of 460 British 'Consuls and Princes' who were massacred at a banquet by the treacherous Saxons. He sought the advice of Merlin who told him to send for the Giant's Dance from 'Kilarus', a mountain in Ireland. Aurelius sent his brother Uther Pendragon and an army of 15,000 men to bring the stones to him, and although they had no problem defeating the native Irish, who quite naturally weren't keen on letting their monument go, actually moving the stones proved an almost impossible task. So Merlin intervened and by using a series of 'engines' he was able to transport them down to the sea and thence by ship to Britain, where they were erected exactly as they had stood in Ireland.

The architect Inigo Jones (1573–1652) was the first person to make a serious study of Stonehenge. He concluded that it had been a Roman temple. In the 18th century the antiquarian and freemason William Stukeley (1687–1765) won overwhelming support for his theory that Stonehenge had in fact been a 'Temple of the British Druids'. Only in the 20th century were archaeologists able to gain an understanding of the monument's real age and arrive at a more realistic assessment of its true purpose.

Numerous prehistoric remains are scattered across the open countryside around Stonehenge. They stand as testimony to the strong collective activity of our distant ancestors, who grazed their cattle, grew their crops, and worshipped their gods on and around Salisbury Plain. In about 3500 BC work was begun to build Stonehenge, which it has been established was built in three phases over a period that spanned around 1,500 years. The first stage was the construction of the circular bank and ditch that contains the Aubrey Holes (named after the 17th-century antiquarian John Aubrey (1626–1697), who included a plan of Stonehenge in his lengthy and discursive *Monumenta Brittanica*). It was at this time that the first of the standing stones was erected outside the single entrance to the circle. The second stage began some 200 or more years later. It was during this phase of the construction that the bluestones were transported to the site from Wales. However, not long afterwards these were taken down and the giant stones that dominate the site today, and which form most peoples' abiding image of Stonehenge, were put in their place. Some of these stones weigh around 26 tons and stand 5.5m (18ft) high by 2m (7ft) wide, so it is safe to assume that a veritable army of workmen must have struggled over their erection. They were evidently skilled craftsmen, for they carved the stones to make them slightly convex, slotted them into place with lintels that covered each of the two vertical stones and then hinged them into place by use of ball and socket joints.

OPPOSITE: *Stonehenge still stands proud and erect on Salisbury Plain, but as Lord Byron astutely observed, 'what the devil is it?'*

These trilithons (so-called because three stones were fitted together) were constructed in the circle and horseshoe shape that is still visible today. Later the dismantled bluestones were repositioned.

Some 1,500 years after the beginning of Stonehenge the final changes took place. The bluestones were dismantled yet again and re-erected inside the circle where they can be seen today, and where they give the distinct impression of cowering beneath the colossal trilithons. At the same time, the stone now known as the Altar Stone, a large block of green sandstone from Milford Haven in Pembrokeshire, was set up in front of one of the trilithons. The thousands of man hours required to move and position the stones, together with the detailed planning, testify to Stonehenge being very important to the peoples of that time. The fact that its designers – and there can be no doubt whatsoever that this is an elaborately designed monument – carefully selected the blue and green stones and then transported them to the site from Wales, is evidence that these stones must have had a particular significance for their people. Stonehenge was evidently not intended as a mere meeting place for the local community, but today any discussion of its original purpose can be little more than speculation. Although a few tantalizing clues do shed a glimmer of light onto what its original function may have been. Cremation burials found in the Aubrey Holes clearly show, for example, that funerary rites were once performed at Stonehenge. It is possible that during the midsummer solstice, the first Stonehenge was intended as a place where the rays of the life-giving sun could shine upon the ancestral remains buried here as it rose between the so-called Heel Stone and another stone that no longer exists, and that the Aubrey Holes were intended to represent entrances into the Underworld. Another theory is that the monument may have been used as a basic calendar to either map the heavenly bodies for religious purposes, or simply to chart the seasons.

Today, Stonehenge is but a shadow of its former glory, although it is still an impressive place. Even though it was abandoned some 3,000 years ago, an aura of enchantment still pervades the whole site. There is a genuine consensus that its function was almost certainly religious, and nobody who has watched the midwinter sunrise over the great sarsen stones at the winter solstice can doubt that the stones must have had some astronomical significance or purpose.

At dawn on the morning of the summer solstice white-robed descendants of the United Ancient Order of Druids (founded by freemasons in London in 1833), still come to the site to perform a ritual handed down through oral tradition, during which

LEFT: *Some of the Stones at Avebury give the distinct impression that they are awakening from a long slumber in order to cast the spell of their ancient magic across their surroundings.*

they play harps and trumpets, salute the Heel Stone and the sarsen stones, utter murmuring chants and wave oak leaves or incense into the air. At other times of the year access to the stones is prevented by a fence intended to protect this ancient monument from the rigours and, sad to say, vandalizing tendencies of the modern tourist industry. Yet this is still a special, mystical and magical place to visit, and if you arrive here in the early morning before the ceaseless onslaught of tourist buses disgorge their cargo onto the site, you can truly experience the sheer spiritual beauty of a place where people came to worship at the dawn of time.

WHITE HORSE, WESTBURY
WILTSHIRE
The Mount of The Ancient Gods

There is considerable debate over the origins of the Westbury White Horse, which has the distinction of being the oldest of Wiltshire's white horses. Its age is difficult to ascertain since it was enthusiastically 'restored' in 1778 by the very aptly named Mr George Gee. There are those who believe that the horse's genesis might belong to the days of the old gods, although this is generally dismissed as fanciful romanticizing. Common consensus holds that the initial carving was made to commemorate King Alfred's victory over the Danes at the battle of Ethandune in AD 878. Historians are divided over whether or not the battle actually took place in this vicinity, and some of them are therefore wont to dismiss this idea, like the horse's ancient heritage, as nothing more than speculation.

The original creature appears to have had a somewhat forlorn and ragged look about it, the despondent appearance being in many ways reminiscent of the Uffington White Horse (see page 46). Mr Gee, who was the steward to Lord Abingdon, set out to make it more horse-like and in so doing he doubled its size. So although he created a competent image of a horse, his etching lacks the otherworldly mysticism that the original appears to have possessed.

That said, it is without doubt an impressive local landmark and its brilliant whiteness is certainly awesome to behold. Its situation on a plunging escarpment is both stirring and inspiring, and the fact it commands attention from miles around moved Charles Tennyson Turner, brother of Alfred, Lord Tennyson, to laud its glories in one of his more effective sonnets:

> As from the Dorset shore I travell'd home
> I saw the charge of the Wiltshire Wold ;
> A far-seen figure, stately to behold,
> Whose groom the shepherd is, the hoe his comb;
> His wizard-spell even sober daylight own'd;
> That night I dream'd him into living will;
> He neigh'd – and, straight, the chalk the chalk pour'd down the hill.

AVEBURY STONE CIRCLES
AVEBURY, WILTSHIRE
Where Man Worshipped at the Dawn of Time

Ancient banks and ditches, almost a mile in circumference, encircle much of the tiny village of Avebury. On them stands Europe's largest stone circle or, to be more precise, several stone circles, dating from between 4000 and 2400 BC. It is a place steeped in mystery, from which the gods that our ancestors worshipped have never really departed.

The modern story of Avebury begins in 1649 when Wiltshireman and antiquarian, John Aubrey (1626–1697), rode into Avebury and 'was wonderfully surprised at the sight of those vast stones, of which I had never heard before.' Aubrey knew instinctively that the stones and the odd earth shapes within which they stood were certainly very old and definitely very special. But this was the age of Cromwell's Protectorate, and ancient monuments such as these were not considered particularly important or noteworthy, and so it would be another 14 years before Aubrey would be able to bring his find to the attention of a wider public.

In 1663, with the monarchy now restored, Aubrey gave Charles II a tour of the site and later that year the first basic maps of the stone circles were displayed at the Royal Society, of which Aubrey was a founder member. Lauding the praises of the magnificent megaliths, or the few at least that were then on display, Aubrey was moved to comment that Avebury 'does as much exceed in greatness the so renowned Stonehenge, as a cathedral doeth a parish church.' Yet over the centuries that followed it would be Stonehenge, not Avebury, that would capture the public imagination and become famous throughout the world.

Yet this, until recently at least, lack of international recognition has proved a blessing in disguise, because Avebury has managed to steer clear of the encroachment of mass tourism that has made Stonehenge little more than a clinical museum piece, roped off to prevent millions of over-enthusiastic hands from inflicting all manner of damage and indignities on its stones. Avebury, by contrast, is a living piece of history around which you can walk at leisure and whose stones you can touch and absorb the ancient energies that you just know crackle within them.

Avebury consists of three stone circles surrounded by an internal ditch and a bank. The bank measures 425m (1,396ft) in diameter and approximately 9m (30ft) high. The largest of the three stone circles is located on the inside of the ditch. Sometimes referred to as the Great Stone Circle it was originally comprised of around 98 stones of which only 27 now remain. Some of these stones weigh as much as 40 tonnes and the effort required to erect them must have been colossal, indicating just how important this site was to the prehistoric tribes. Two smaller rings, each made up of between 27 and 29 stones, of which only four and five respectively now survive, stand inside the Great Stone Circle. The Great Circle has four entrances, from the South Entrance you are able to see a double row of stones referred to as Kennet Avenue. This avenue originally ran for about one mile Southwards passing the village of West Kennet and ending at the Sanctuary on Overton Hill.

There can be little doubt that Avebury served as a religious and ceremonial centre, although any knowledge about the beliefs and rituals celebrated there have long since been forgotten. Of course such a massive and impressive testimony to the old gods could not go unchallenged when Christianity began to establish its dominance. In the 14th century, probably acting on the instructions of the Church, the villagers of Avebury began to topple the megaliths and bury them in deep pits. This zealous act of vandalism angered whatever spirits lurked within the stones and they exacted vengeance on at least one of their assailants. When the monoliths were rediscovered in 1938, several 14th-century coins, and sundry other items, were found buried beneath one of them. The archaeologists had little problem identifying the last owner of these objects, because his grinning skull was leering back at them from beneath the massive stone! It would seem that a tragic accident had caused the colossus to topple onto the unfortunate man crushing him to death. The sheer weight of the stone had made removal of his body impossible, and so his 14th-century workmates had simply left him there. Since the tools found alongside his bones suggested he was a barber-surgeon,

the murderous megalith became known as the 'Barber Stone' and today stands proud and erect upon its original site.

In the 18th century the descendants of those medieval villagers began breaking up the remaining stones to use them for building material. It wasn't until the 1930s, when wealthy Scotsman Alexander Keiller, began purchasing houses and land in and around the village that many of the stones began to see the light of day again. Trees were torn down, houses demolished and gradually the stone circles of Avebury began to awake from their long slumber. It is testimony to Keiller's determination and foresight that the circles are today so well preserved, and it is thanks to his vision that their reconstruction has once more made it possible to gain an impression of the sheer magnitude of the stones.

Today, Avebury remains a special and enchanting place. The stones still inspire feelings of wonder, and no one who gazes upon them for the first time, or arrives to find them rising ghost-like from a swirling mist on a crisp winters morning, can fail to be moved by their magic.

SILBURY HILL
Nr. Marlborough, Wiltshire
A Monument to Bygone Engineering

This awe-inspiring wonder is the largest man-made mound in Europe. It dates from around 2700 BC, is 40m (130ft) high and covers an area of five and a half acres. It has been estimated that it would have taken 700 men, 10 years of continuous labour to fashion the 12 million cubic feet of earth, chalk and

stone into the breathtaking monument that confronts us today. Yet no one knows why it was built or even what purpose it originally served. Was it a military stronghold? Could it have been an ancient burial mound, a primitive observatory, or a depiction of the pregnant earth goddess?

With so much uncertainty surrounding its origins, numerous scientific and archaeological theories have been put forward in a forlorn hope of both explaining and understanding it. Local tradition, meanwhile, has added its own rich smattering of lore and legend to the debate. One tale has it that the Devil was on his way to dump a huge sack of earth onto the citizens of Marlborough, when the Druid Priests at nearby Avebury used their magic to stop him. Unable to reach his goal, the Devil emptied the earth from his sack and thus created Silbury Hill. There is another long-held tradition that the hill is the grave of a king whose name was *Sil*. He is said to be at the centre of the mound, clothed in a golden suit of armour, astride a horse that is also clad in gold. Needless to say, with such potential riches possibly lying within, Silbury Hill has been subjected to numerous archaeological excavations but nothing of note has ever been discovered and it remains a mystifying memorial to a bygone and forgotten people.

WEST KENNET LONG BARROW
Nr. Marlborough, Wiltshire
England's Largest Long Barrow

This truly impressive Neolithic tomb stands on a prominent chalk ridge and stretches for over 97m (320ft), making it the largest long barrow in England. Its construction was begun around 3600 BC, thus it predates both Stonehenge and Avebury. The barrow was used as a place of internment for over a thousand years, and then the Beaker People sealed it, by filling the passage and chamber to the roof with earth and flint, and then placing huge sarsen stones across its entrance. This was done either in the hope of keeping the spirits inside contained, or else to prevent abuse of so sacred a place by marauding bands of grave robbers. This filling in, however, didn't stop a 17th-century physician, Dr R. Tope, from burrowing into the mound and removing several human bones ,which he then proceeded to grind into a powder that he mixed into his medicines.

In 1859, and again between 1955 and 1956, a more scientific and sensitive archaeological excavation was carried out and this found evidence for a total of 46 burials. These included men, women and children, all of whom had been laid to rest in what has been described as 'a womb from which the dead ancestors could be reborn'. There is a local tradition that at sunrise on Midsummer's Day a spectral priest dressed in white walks into the mound accompanied by a red-eared hound. This may well be a distant folk memory of some long ago ritualistic event that once took place at the barrow.

West Kennet Long Barrow is a place of contrasts. The stones that adorn its interior are graceful with their elegant swoops and delicate curves. Unfortunately, untold damage has been done by the irresponsible actions of some visitors who have an overwhelming desire to light candles and incense by the stones supposedly to add to the aura of mysticism that surrounds the ancient site. This is, to say the least, destructive to the stones and is also totally unnecessary, for to catch the stones in the early morning as the sun rises over the landscape, or to return to them at close of day as it sinks behind the horizon, is to find yourself centuries removed from the pressures of the modern age, and the magic of the barrow needs no candles or votive offerings in order to touch the soul and fire the imagination.

ABOVE: *At sunrise on Midsummer's Day local tradition holds that a spectral priest walks into the mound of West Kennet Long Barrow. Could this be a folk memory of some long ago ritualistic event held here?*

OPPOSITE: *Silbury Hill is the largest man made mound in Europe and stands as a proud testimony to the skills of the ancient people who constructed it.*

Stony Kings,
Whispering Knights and
Neolithic Remnants

✵

WE DO LIE BENEATH THE GRASS
IN THE MOONLIGHT, IN THE SHADE
OF THE YEW-TREE. THEY THAT PASS
HEAR US NOT. WE ARE AFRAID
THEY WOULD ENVY OUR DELIGHT,
IN OUR GRAVES BY GLOW-WORM NIGHT.
COME FOLLOW US, AND SMILE AS WE;
WE SAIL TO THE ROCK IN THE ANCIENT WAVES,
WHERE THE SNOW FALLS BY THOUSANDS INTO THE SEA,
AND THE DROWNED AND THE SHIPWRECKED HAVE HAPPY GRAVES.

SIBILLA'S DIRGE
BY THOMAS LOVELL BEDOES (1803 - 1849).

HEREFORDSHIRE, GLOUCESTERSHIRE & OXFORDSHIRE

The landscape from Oxfordshire to Herefordshire is both physically and psychically varied. It offers those who seek Britain's mysterious past a veritable cornucopia of history, myth and legend. Here you will find the reclusive and weather-beaten Rollright Stones, a Neolithic monument that legend has chosen to remember as a king and his army turned to stone by a cunning witch; and the quiet ruins of Hailes Abbey, once an important place of pilgrimage. Then there is the tranquillity and beauty of the Cotswolds, where you can gaze upon ancient burial mounds left behind by a long-forgotten people. However, this region is also a battle-scarred landscape where many events of national importance have occurred, and has long been known as 'England's cockpit'. Here Charles I established his headquarters in the dark days of the Civil War. Through here the Saxons drove the native Britons into the brooding mountains of Wales, and began a struggle for mastery of southern England that would last for 600 years. Today, the roar of battle has given way to the increasingly noisy hum of the car, and the tramping of troops has been replaced by the steady plod of thousands of ramblers enjoying the fresh country air of some of England's most beautiful and tranquil countryside.

KEY

1. Arthur's Stone
2. The Church of St Mary
   and St David
3. Uley Long Barrow
4. Hailes Abbey
5. Belas Knap Long Barrow
6. Wayland's Smithy
7. White Horse
8. Rollright Stones

ARTHUR'S STONE
Nr. Dorstone, Herefordshire
Where Arthur Fought a Giant

According to legend, Arthur's Stone marks the spot where King Arthur fought with a king or a giant, and having broken his adversary's back, buried him at this site marking his resting place with the stones. Some claim that the cup marks that can be seen on the stones are the indentations left by the giant's elbows as he hit the ground. Others maintain that they are the dents left by Arthur's knees as he knelt in prayer to give thanks for his victory. In reality this sullen group of stones are the remains of a Neolithic tomb that dates from around 3700 to 2700 BC. Its mighty 25-ton capstone is supported by nine uprights which give the distinct impression that they are finding it a struggle to support their heavy load.

PAGE 38: *The Sheela-Na-Gig carving on Kilpek Church might be a fertility symbol or a graphic warning against the sins of the flesh.*

PAGE 39: *The setting of Gloucestershire's Hailes Abbey is as peaceful and spiritually uplifting as you could ever wish to find.*

ABOVE: *Legend has ousted the spirits of the former occupants of this Neolithic tomb and replaced them with the spirit of King Arthur who is said to have once fought a ferocious giant at the site.*

A tomb such as this was used as a communal burial vault and would no doubt have housed the dead of several generations. Although the mound that once covered the tomb has now been almost worn away, it is still possible to imagine just how important the burial of their dead was to the Neolithic farmers who constructed the tomb. After all, to have hauled the gigantic capstone onto its supports would have taken considerable effort with only the rudimentary tools that were available to them. They evidently considered the challenge worthwhile and intended this to remain as a lasting monument to their ancestors.

THE CHURCH OF ST MARY AND ST DAVID
Kilpeck, Herefordshire
A Lewd Lady of Mysterious Origins

Kilpeck church blends harmoniously into its surrounding landscape of rolling fields and tree-covered hills. It is a peaceful little building dating from the 12th century, whose crowning glory is a south doorway around which a stunning array of pagan and Christian motifs, etched into the delicate sandstone, survive as a lasting testimony to the humour and skills of the craftsmen, who created them almost a thousand years ago. Each exquisite carving – be it of a mysterious warrior, a writhing snake, a pagan green man or any one of the numerous real or imaginary beasts – serves as a vivid reminder of the beliefs, fears and aspirations of our ancestors.

Perhaps the most controversial and enigmatic of the figures is that of the Sheela-Na-Gig which is located on the south wall of the apse.

The name Sheela-Na-Gig is a collective one which is used to describe over a hundred such carvings that are found predominantly on churches but also other important buildings all over England and Ireland. They depict naked females posed in a manner that displays and emphasizes their genitalia. The name Sheela-Na-Gig is of Irish origin and is possibly derived from a common Gaelic expression meaning an immodest woman. She has been variously described as a device to ward of evil spirits, a sexual stimulant, an obscene old hag, a fertility symbol or a depiction of the Mother Goddess.

There is a common consensus that the Sheela-Na-Gig was a Christian invention, which incorporated Celtic symbolism. Certainly, the almost triangular head and the huge round eyes are reminiscent of early Celtic art. It has been suggested that the medieval Church may have allowed a powerful pre-Christian figure to coexist with its own imagery, or even that it adopted this exhibitionist female as

OPPOSITE: *Numerous pagan symbols are to be found carved around the exquisite south doorway at Kilpeck Church.*

BELOW: *Crawl into the cramped interior of Uley Long Barrow and the stresses and strains of our modern age dissolve into the darkness that envelopes you.*

a means of warning against the sins of the flesh. Another widely held belief, particularly in Ireland, maintains that she is intended as a fertility symbol. Yet although her wide-open legs and exaggerated vulva imply fertility, there is a strange paradox in that the upper half of the figure is either shown as being flat-chested, or else having long drooping breasts suggesting extreme old age. In other words, she could be taken as a symbol of either fertility or infertility, while the disproportionately large head is always bald and could represent both birth and death.

The truth is we will never know for sure why the craftsmen chose to adorn so many sacred buildings with overtly pagan and seemingly obscene imagery. Perhaps our desire to believe in ancient symbolism and to tarnish our ancestors with our modern ideals have blinded us to what may have been nothing more than a medieval joke from a bawdier and far more down-to-earth age than ours.

ULEY LONG BARROW (HETTY PEGLAR'S TUMP)
NR. DURSLEY, GLOUCESTERSHIRE
A Passageway to Another Realm

The local name for a long barrow is a *tump*, and Hetty Peglar's Tump, or Uley Long Barrow as it is also known, is named after Hester Peggler, the 17th-century landowner's wife. However, this curious and mysterious place is far older than that and dates back to around 3000 BC. It consists of a

mysticism. But catch it on your own and the effect upon your senses, both physical and spiritual, is pure magic. As you crouch alone in this dark womb, the world outside seems to drift further and further away and it doesn't take a great leap of the imagination to understand how some people have come to see this as an entrance to another realm, or even a doorway into fairyland. It would come as little surprise if you crawled out to find that time had stood still within the tump but days have gone by outside!

HAILES ABBEY
NR. WINCHCOMBE, GLOUCESTERSHIRE
A Tranquil Slice of Rural Paradise

The ruins of Hailes Abbey teeter in quiet seclusion on the western fringe of the Cotswolds and enjoy a beautiful and tranquil setting surrounded by lush pasture and woodland. It was founded in 1246 by Richard, Earl of Cornwall, brother of Henry III. When caught in a storm at sea and his ship showed every sign of sinking, Richard cried out to God that if his life was spared he would found a religious house. His prayers were answered and upon returning to land he set about keeping his vow. Henry granted him the manor of Hailes and five years later, with the help of the Cistercians, his Hailes Abbey loomed over this delightful slice of rural Gloucestershire. In 1251, Henry III, Queen Eleanor of Provence and 13 bishops attended the consecration ceremony.

The abbey would probably have remained a lovely though relatively

passage with two chambers on either side and an end chamber. To enter it you need to drop down onto your hands and knees, and crawl into its dark interior, where a torch is an absolute necessity if you are to be able to appreciate the stonework inside. The site itself can be quite busy and this in turn detracts somewhat from its aura of unimportant place had the monks not, in around 1270, gained possession of a phial said to contain some of Christ's blood. Having such a potent religious artefact enabled the abbey to become a pilgrimage centre and as its wealth increased it expanded accordingly. A special extension to the east end of the abbey church was built, and there the phial was kept in a shrine. Soon Hailes had become one of the most popular pilgrimage destinations in England, and the faithful flocked in their thousands to pay homage to the sacred phial. The prior even built a 'hotel' to accommodate the more demanding, wealthier visitors and to attend to their more earthly needs. This hotel still survives as the George Hotel in Winchecombe. The abbey was closed down in 1539, during the Dissolution of the Monasteries, and the phial, which had brought the pilgrims along the dusty byways for centuries, was smashed. The so-called 'blood of Christ' was found to be nothing more a than mixture of saffron and honey.

Hailes Abbey today is a tranquil place of tottering arches around which sheep graze contentedly. Because it is not high on tourist itineraries, it is often possible to have the ruins all to yourself. In those moments of solitude you can truly appreciate the site's pervading sense of peace and tranquillity.

BELAS KNAP LONG BARROW
Nr. Winchecombe, Gloucestershire
Where 40 Souls were Laid to Rest
Belas Knap is a truly impressive Neolithic long barrow approximately 54m (178ft) long by 18m (60ft) wide, that stands as a proud and enduring monument to the architectural skill and cultural erudition of our distant ancestors. It boasts a false entrance at the north end and four burial chambers. The remains of nearly 40 people were found

in excavations carried out at the site between 1863 and 1865 and again between 1928 and 1930, along with other remains including part of a boar's tusk pendant. The word barrow, incidentally, comes from the Anglo-Saxon word *beorg*, which is related to *berg*, meaning 'mountain'.

WAYLAND'S SMITHY
Nr. Ashbury, Oxfordshire
The Magical Smith
As you stumble along the Neolithic track known as the Ridgeway, you pass by a sylvan hilltop grotto, where a circle of ancient trees stand, sentry-like, around a mysterious mound that exudes an aura of brooding detachment and which has long been known as Wayland's Smithy. Its origins stretch back over 5,000 years when a prehistoric people constructed a burial chamber on this windswept crest. Around 3300 BC a new wave of people arrived at the site, evicted the earlier residents and built over their tomb with a larger more imposing earthwork. Four thousand years later, Saxon settlers stumbled upon the ancient relic and, mystified as to its origins, attributed it to their god Weland the Smith.

OPPOSITE: *The secluded remnants of Hailes Abbey look back on a long lost age of spirituality and contemplation.*

BELOW: *The remains of nearly 40 people have been found during excavations and Belas Knapp, testimony to its bygone importance as a place of internment.*

Weland, or Wayland as he became known, was the Saxon adaptation of the Norse Volundr, who was a magical smith of such outstanding skill that King Nidudr captured him and, having lamed him to prevent his escape, set him to work at the royal forge. Volundr exacted a dreadful revenge upon his tormentor. First, he lured the King's two sons to the forge, murdered them and fashioned their skulls into drinking vessels, which he then sent to their father. Next, when the King's daughter came to ask that he mend a ring, he drugged and raped the unfortunate girl. Then, using his magical powers, he escaped by flying through the air, pausing only to taunt the anguished monarch as he passed overhead.

The smith's revenge was a well-known Saxon tale and is referred to in several Old English poems, including the 10th-century *Deor* and the heroic epic *Waldere*, dating from around AD 1000, and which mentions both Weland and Widia, his son by the princess. It can also be seen in pictographic form on the much earlier Frank's Casket (now in the British Museum), which was probably carved in Northumbria in the 8th century.

The association of the hillside tomb with the god Weland was certainly established by the 9th century, because a Berkshire Charter dated AD 855 actually mentions it as *Welandes Smidde*. Over succeeding centuries the fearsome reputation of the mound's legendary occupant gave way to a gentler more constructive persona, and by 1738 the antiquarian Francis Wise recorded the tradition: 'At this place lived formerly an invisible Smith, and if a traveller's horse had lost a Shoe upon the road, he had no more to do than to bring the Horse to this place with a piece of money, and leaving both their for some little time, he might come again and find the money gone, but the Horse new shod.'

As recently as the 19th century, children would visit Wayland's Smithy and listen with baited breath for the pounding of his hammer, which they were assured could often be heard sounding from within the tumulus. Even today, standing before the mysterious passageway that dips between its ancient walls of stone, and then disappears into a heavy wedge of ancient rock, you can easily feel yourself to be on the threshold of some hidden kingdom, where ancient gods hold court and the magic of bygone times hangs heavy in the air.

THE WHITE HORSE
UFFINGTON, OXFORDSHIRE
A Dragon or a Horse?
Standing next to the ancient Ridgeway Path, the Uffington White Horse is the oldest and one of the most impressive hill-figures in Britain. It is 114m (374ft) in length and its origins are shrouded in mystery. It has a melancholic and timeless aura, and the brilliant whiteness of the chalk from which it is carved lends the almost shorthand-like depiction of the horse a quality that is as haunting as it is impressive.

The general consensus is that the White Horse is anywhere between 2,000 and 3,000 years old. Theories as to its original purpose include that it was the tribal emblem of the Belgae who occupied Uffington fort on the hilltop above, or that it is a depiction of the Celtic horse-goddess Epona. Some say that it is not a horse at all but rather a representation of the dragon slain by St George on the amazingly flat summit of Dragon Hill, which cowers in the valley beneath the enigmatic creature.

Until the 19th century the horse was ritually scoured every seven years. This evolved into a three-day festival consisting of festivities and games that included traditional cheese rolling, wrestling and many other activities. The fête has not taken place for around a hundred years and the horse is now maintained by English Heritage.

Although the climb to the horse can be exhausting, and the elegant grace of its curves and swirls are difficult to appreciate from close up, the hillside that the white horse occupies is a truly magical spot from which to contemplate the beautiful landscape around you. The Iron Age fort of Uffington Castle is visible on the hill above, while in the valley below is the mystical splendour of Dragon Hill and, keeping watch over them, is the White Horse – a silent guardian that has stood here since the days before the English nation existed and which will no doubt still be here long after it is no more.

THE ROLLRIGHT STONES
NR. LONG COMPTON, OXFORDSHIRE
The King and His Men
These ancient and mystical stones, standing upon a hill that overlooks the village of Long Compton, have a curious legend woven around their origins. One day, so the story goes, a king set out to conquer the land, but when he came to the summit of the hill above Long Compton he met with a witch who told him:

Seven long strides shalt thou take
And if Long Compton then can'st see
King of England thou shalt be.

The king, safe in the knowledge that the exposed hilltop afforded an excellent and uninterrupted view of the village beneath sneered back:

OPPOSITE: *Guarded by a ring of skeletal trees Wayland's Smithy is one of those places where the old magic lives on unmolested by the passage of time.*

Stick, stock, stone
As King of England I shall be known.

Confidently, he took seven strides forward, only to find his view obstructed by a huge mound. Turning back to the chortling hag, he heard her chant:

As Long Compton thou can'st not see
King of England thou shalt not be
Rise up stick, stand still stone
For King of England thou shall be none
Thou and thy men hoar stones shall be
And I myself, an elder tree.

And so the King was turned to stone, and can still be seen on the peaceful hillside above the village. Nearby, stands a larger circle of between 60 and 80 stones, said to be the King's Army and which, it is claimed, can never be accurately counted since no two attempts will ever yield the same total. Indeed, there is a somewhat alarming tradition that should anyone succeed in counting the same number three times, then they will be struck dead on the spot! On the edge of a nearby field stand five larger stones huddled together in a conspiratorial formation. They are known as the 'Whispering Knights' and are said to have been five warriors who were plotting against the king when the witch's spell fell upon them.

Legends aside, the Rollright Stones are in reality a Neolithic stone circle dating from between 2500 and 2000 BC. Although lacking the dramatic appearance of such circles as Stonehenge and Avebury their appeal is no less mysterious. It is their reclusiveness which lends them such an aura of enchantment.

There are also stories about the consequences of moving or damaging the Stones. A young soldier is said to have once taken a chipping from one of them to India with him, and no sooner had he arrived than he promptly died of typhus. Another story tells how a local farmer removed the capstone of the Whispering Knights to build a bridge across a stream. It took many horses to drag the stone down the hill and two men were killed in the struggle to haul the monolith across the stream. Once it was in place the farmer was horrified by eerie noises that plagued his every hour. Each morning he would discover that the stone had mysteriously turned over during the night and he would have to lift it back from where it lay on the bank. Finally admitting defeat, he decided to return the stone and was surprised to find that it was easily dragged back to its rightful place by just one horse.

LEFT: *The Rollright Stones might seem a little ragged and forlorn at first glance, but people return time and again to absorb their energies and ponder the mysteries that surround them.*

Capital Miracles and Holy Shrines

The soul's dark cottage, batter'd and decay'd.
Lets in new light through chinks that Time hath made:
Stronger by weakness, wiser men become
As they draw near to their eternal home.
Leaving the old, both worlds at once they view
That stand upon the threshold of the new.

FROM 'OLD AGE'
BY EDMUND WALLER (1606–1687)

50

Buckinghamshire, Bedfordshire Hertfordshire & London

ell is a city much like London… A Populous and smoky city' wrote the poet Shelley, no doubt summing up the feelings and attitudes of the millions of citizens to whom the metropolis has been home over the centuries. It can be an overwhelming city to live and work in, a fast-paced, impersonal place where no one has time for anyone else and the past is buried beneath a seemingly endless tide of modern construction, which, at times, can make the nation's capital seem nothing more than a continuous building site. Yet there is plenty to reward those who care to scratch this superficial surface. For London is, in certain respects, a very spiritual and mystical place. To stray a few short feet from Fleet Street, for example, is to enter the

Inns of Court, the squares and courtyards of which have changed little in several hundred years. A short distance away is the Priory Church of St Bartholomew the Great, built in 1123 and literally founded on a vision. Outside the capital you have some delightful countryside and truly mysterious places. Chief amongst these must surely be the

PAGE 50: Stevington Holy Well is a pagan shrine that later became a place of Christian pilgrimage.

PREVIOUS PAGE: Elstow's Abbey Church of St Mary and St Helena motivated John Bunyan to write his inspirational tome, Pilgrim's Progress.

KEY

1. Sir John Shorne's Well
2. Stevington Holy Well
3. The Abbey Church of of St Mary and St Helena
4. Royston Cave
5. St Mary's Church
6. St Albans Cathedral
7. Temple of Mithras
8. Priory Church of St Bartholomew
9. Temple Church

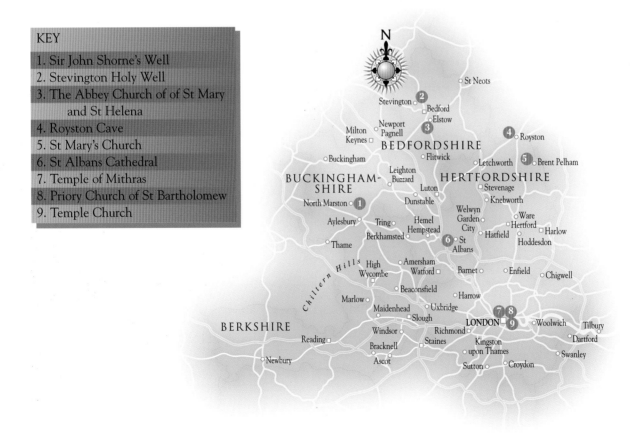

Royston Cave, discovered by accident in the 18th century and a place whose origins will never really be known. All in all this is a region that offers a rich mix of mystical lore, and one that is an absolute pleasure to explore.

SIR JOHN SHORNE'S WELL
NORTH MARSTON, BUCKINGHAMSHIRE
The Healing Waters of Yesteryear

Sir John Shorne was the parish rector for North Marston between 1290 and 1315. During a particularly harsh drought he is said to have saved his parishioners by striking the ground with his staff and causing a spring of crystal clear water to gush forth. It soon became common knowledge that the well possessed curative properties, and as its fame spread, pilgrims flocked to the shrine that grew up around it. The majority came to drink its waters, but it also appears to have been used as a bath for invalids. The spring itself was said to never freeze or fail, and the well was renowned both for its remarkable purity and for the extreme coldness of its water. Today, a somewhat unsightly stone enclosure, topped by a hefty wooden door, covers the well that sits about 140m (450ft) away from the parish church of St Mary's. It might not look as impressive as it once did, and it might be difficult

BELOW: *Sir John Shorne's Well was once an important place of pilgrimage. Its waters were said to never freeze or fail.*

to see what it was that attracted our ancestors to places such as this, but it has a certain ethereal quality, which coupled with the sense of history that surrounds it, makes it a worthwhile site at which to while away a few moments.

STEVINGTON HOLY WELL
STEVINGTON, BEDFORDSHIRE
The Pilgrim's Progress

Stevington is a pleasant stone-built village at the centre of which stands a 14th-century cross. It was at this cross in John Bunyan's (1628–1688) *The Pilgrim's Progress* that Christian lost his burden. 'He ran thus till he came at a place somewhat ascending: and upon that place stood a cross, and a little below, in the bottom, a sepulchre. So I saw in my dream that, just as Christian came up with the cross, his burden loosed from off his shoulders, and fell from off his back and began to tumble; and so continued to do till it came to the mouth of the sepulchre, where it fell in, and I saw it no more.'

Bunyan may well have had the village's Holy Well in mind when he wrote those lines. It is situated below the boundary wall of the village churchyard, and its cool waters pour from the rock on which the church stands. It is believed that the well was originally a pagan shrine that was Christianized as the old deities were absorbed into the new religion. By the Middle Ages it had become a popular place of pilgrimage and it was widely believed that its waters could

THE HOLY OR SCHORNE WELL

FOUNDED BY MASTER JOHN SCHORNE, VICAR OF ST. MARY'S CHURCH, NORTH MARSTON, 1290–1314. THE WATER HAD HEALING PROPERTIES AND THE WELL WAS VISITED BY MANY PILGRIMS.

'JOHN SCHORNE, GENTLEMAN BORNE, CONJURED THE DEVIL INTO A BOOT.'

LOCAL JINGLE

never freeze or dry up. However, not all those who came here in search of a cure had their prayers answered. Indeed, the Fair Maid of Kent, Joan, wife of the Black Prince, is said to have died here in 1386.

THE ABBEY CHURCH OF ST MARY AND ST HELENA
ELSTOW, BEDFORDSHIRE
John Bunyan The Mystical Visionary

John Bunyan (1628–1688), the son of a tinker, was christened in the church of St Mary and St Helena on 30th November 1628. He grew up through the troubled years that culminated in the English Civil War. While still in his teens he fought for the Parliamentarians against the Royalists. In 1646 he returned to Elstow and married a local girl with whom he settled down to raise a family, which he supported by working as a tinker. His favourite pastimes included dancing and playing 'tipcat', which was a popular Bedfordshire game in which a player strikes a small piece of wood from a hole in the ground and, as it rises, hits it again as far as he can. But when his wife gave birth to a blind daughter, Bunyan began to reflect seriously on his life. By his own later admission he had few equals in 'cursing, swearing, lying and blaspheming the Holy name of God'. He began to feel the need to find a deeper purpose as the religious scruples that had plagued his childhood returned.

One of Bunyan's great pleasures was ringing the bells in the church's curiously detached tower, and the fifth bell of the chime is still called the 'Bunyan Bell' in the belief that he once rang it. He became convinced that this activity was sinful and, so tradition has it, took to ringing the bell from the safety of the doorway for fear that the tower would fall on his head as punishment. A groove in the plaster over the doorway used to be pointed out as having been worn by the bell rope as he sheltered from possible divine retribution. Then, one Sunday afternoon as he played tipcat on the village green, he suddenly heard a voice 'dart from heaven into my soul which said "wilt thou leave thy sins and go to heaven or have thy sins and go to hell?"' Spurred to action, Bunyan joined a small independent congregation that met at St John's Church, Bedford where he discovered to his amazement that he was a gifted preacher.

Following the restoration of the monarchy in 1660, the authorities were convinced that national unity was only achievable through religious uniformity, and they forbade independent preachers. Bunyan, however, refused to be silenced, was arrested and spent 12 years in Bedford gaol.

OPPOSITE: *Holy wells, such as the one at Stevington, were once pagan shrines that were Christianised as the church began to incorporate older religions by absorbing them into their own beliefs and rituals.*

Since he was not a common felon he was afforded several privileges and it was in prison that he composed his great spiritual allegory *The Pilgrim's Progress*. Several locations around Bedfordshire were incorporated into the narrative, including the abbey church whose bells Bunyan had so delighted in ringing.

Elstow Parish Church possessed an old gate through which, as a boy, Bunyan must have passed every Sunday. He remembers it in *The Pilgrim's Progress,* when Christian sets out on his journey and is unsure of the way to the Celestial City. However, he meets Evangelist and asks him to direct him. Evangelist points across a wide field and asks him if he can see 'yonder wicket gate'. Christian cannot see it so Evangelist asks 'Do you see yonder shining light?' (The Light of Christ). When Christian replies that he can, Evangelist advises 'Keep that light in your eye and you will come to the gate'. Christian does as he is advised and sure enough arrives at the gate over which is written, 'Knock and it will be opened unto you'. He knocks and is answered by the gate's keeper, Goodwill, who opens the gate and points him to the straight and narrow path that leads to the Celestial City.

The bell tower, which stands a little way off from the main body of the church, became the strong castle from which Beelzebub 'and they that are with him, shoot arrows at them that come up to this gate; if haply they may die before they enter in'.

Bunyan was released from prison in 1672 and, following a further brief spell of imprisonment, published *The Pilgrim's Progress* in 1678 which was an immediate success. Despite producing a further 40 books by the time of his death in 1688, it is for writing *The Pilgrim's Progress* that he is now best remembered. Inside the church of St Mary and St Helena the font at which he was christened is still used today and visitors can marvel at the stunning, stained-glass window that depicts Christian's journey, and which stands as a colourful testimony to the memory of Elstow's most legendary son.

ROYSTON CAVE
ROYSTON, HERTFORDSHIRE
A Mysterious Cavern in the Centre of Town

In August 1742 workmen set about digging a hole to provide footings for a new bench that was to stand in Royston's Butter Market. Their labours were abruptly halted when their spades and picks struck against what turned out to be a buried millstone. They began to dig around it to give themselves a little leverage with which to prise the object out of their way. But as they did so, they uncovered a shaft that led downwards into the chalk. Mystified as to what exactly it was that they had uncovered, they lowered a young boy into the shaft. He was followed by a 'thin man' who arrived in the cavity shortly after the boy. They found themselves standing in a bell-shaped cavern that was more than half filled with earth.

Word soon spread of the curious find, and citizens of the little market town began flocking to the site in order that they might examine the hole and discuss its function. The most popular theory was that there was probably buried treasure beneath the soil, and spurred on by the thought of the riches that might be awaiting them, the people of Royston began working eagerly around the clock in order that they might clear away the debris. In the process they removed several cartloads of earth. However, to their disappointment all that they found was a chilly, dark cave the walls of which were adorned with numerous strange and indecipherable carvings. Dejected, many of the citizens headed for home.

Those citizens of Royston may have been disappointed at their failure to uncover treasure, but they had in fact stumbled upon something unique in Britain. For the cave, despite recent problems with flooding, is today one of Britain's most unusual tourist attractions. Visitors arrive from all over the world to gaze in wonder at the curious pagan and Christian symbols that adorn its walls. There are depictions of St Christopher and of the Crucifixion. St Lawrence is shown at his martyrdom being roasted on a grill. St Catherine is portrayed being broken on a wheel. There are knights and crosses, as well as an abundance of swords, sun-wheels and hands holding hearts. There is even that most curious of symbols, a Sheela-Na-Gig (see page 43). Yet nobody knows for certain who was responsible for making these curious carvings, exactly how old the chamber is or what its original purpose was.

There is speculation that the cave may be the remnants of a Neolithic flint mine, or that it might have started out as a Roman sepulchre. One theory holds that it was used in the Middle Ages as a hermit's cell. In recent years it has been suggested that the carvings were the work of the Knights Templar, the military religious order who held a weekly market in Royston in the 12th and 13th centuries. They would most certainly have needed a cool place in which to store their produce and this underground chasm would have proved ideal. The cave was, apparently, divided into two storeys by a wooden floor and the knights may have used one section as a chapel to use for their devotions. There is even a theory that the order used it for initiation purposes. The fact that some of the imagery does appear to depict events in Templar history would seem to lend weight to their having some involvement with the cave.

Whatever its origins and original purpose Royston Cave remains a fascinating and mysterious place. No one who stands in its chilly interior and gazes upon the enigmatic carvings and depictions can fail to be moved by the experience.

ST MARY'S CHURCH
BRENT PELHAM, HERTFORDSHIRE
Piers the Dragon Slayer

Piers Shonks lies buried in the north wall of the church of St Mary's in the village of Brent Pelham. Legend has it that one day he went away on holiday and returned to find that a dragon was wreaking havoc on the local community, with the result that the crops lay burnt and ruined in the fields. Determined to rid the district of this fearsome monster, Piers Shonks hunted it down to its nearby lair and following a ferocious and bloody battle he managed to thrust his lance into the dragon's jaws, killing the creature outright. As he stood surveying his handiwork he became puzzled as to why the air still smelt sulphurous, and turning round he was astonished to find the Devil standing behind him, eyeing him with evil intent. Satan, it seems, was beside himself with fury at the loss of his pet, and there and then he vowed that when the bold knight finally breathed his last, he would take his revenge by claiming his soul for eternity. And lest Piers Shonks thought he could evade his satanic majesty's revenge by seeking the protection of the church, the great adversary tersely informed him that he would have his soul whether he was lying inside or outside the church. Shonks, however, was

ABOVE: *Royston Chapel is home to some extremely curious carvings, both pagan and Christian. There are many theories as to who created them, and why.*

OPPOSITE: *Elstow Church enjoys a peaceful and tranquil location. In the days when he cursed and blasphemed, John Bunyan used to enjoy ringing the church bells here.*

made of stern stuff and, unmoved by Old Nick's threats and promises, he shrugged his shoulders and retorted that his soul belonged to God, and the Devil would have a hard job claiming it. With that he stomped back to his manor house and proceeded to lead a long and fruitful life.

Many years later, when Shonks lay upon his deathbed, the Devil's threat began to play upon his mind. So taking his bow he fired an arrow high into the air, and asked that he be laid to rest where it fell. The arrow struck against the north wall of St Mary's church, and so when he died he was entombed in the wall, which meant that he was neither inside nor outside the church and safe from Satan's clutches.

His 11th-century tomb is still visible today on the north wall of the church and upon it is a depiction of the slain dragon. Of course, we no longer believe that dragons ever existed, and are inclined to dismiss such tales as amusing legends to be dismissed out of hand. It is difficult for us to appreciate the inspirational effect that such stories would have had upon our ancestors. For the tomb of Piers Shonks and the legend that surrounds it serves as a reminder that no matter how insurmountable the problems that beset our everyday existence might seem, with faith we can conquer them and rise above our troubles.

BELOW: *Piers Shonks, dragon-slayer extraordinaire, is buried in the wall of St Mary's Church Brent Pelham, to thwart the Devil's attempts to claim his soul.*

ST ALBANS CATHEDRAL
St Albans, Hertfordshire
The First English Martyr

To really get the feel of St Albans you should stand on the site of the Roman city of Verulamium and look over at the hill on which stands the Norman tower of the magnificent abbey. The City of St Albans is not built on the site of its Roman predecessor, because Verulamium was destroyed by the Saxons. However, when the Saxons converted to Christianity they wanted to honour the memory of St Alban, the first English martyr, and so on the hill which overlooked Verulamium where he met his death they built a little chapel, and there, according to the Venerable Bede (c.673–735) 'sick people are healed and great miracles take place to this day'. Two centuries later King Offa II of Mercia founded a Benedictine monastery on the site. The present abbey with its long nave, and tower built of Roman tiles and bricks was constructed by the Normans and begun in 1077.

Alban was a Roman citizen of Verulamium at the beginning of the fourth century. When the Emperor Severus began persecuting Christians, a priest known later as Amphibalus sought refuge in Alban's villa. The priest's devotions and faith greatly intrigued his host, and it wasn't long before he had converted Alban to the Christian faith. One day Alban was warned that soldiers were about to search his villa, and so he donned the priest's garments himself, whilst Amphibalus made good his escape disguised as Alban.

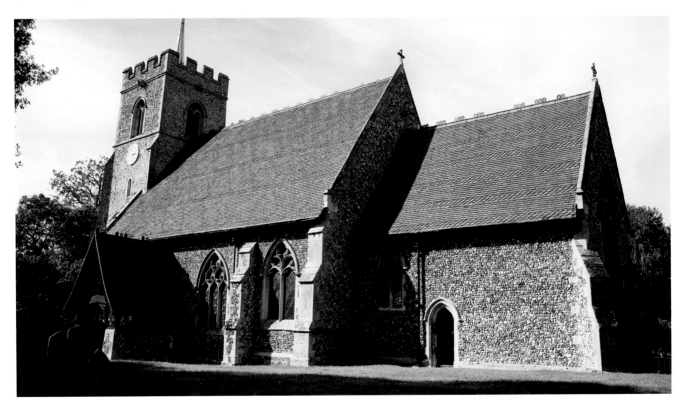

Alban was brought before a magistrate who, furious at the deception, ordered that Alban should receive the punishment due to the priest, if he had indeed become a Christian. Alban declared his Christian faith, saying in words still used as a prayer: 'I worship and adore the true and living God, who created all things.' Despite being scourged by his accusers, Alban refused to sacrifice to the Roman gods and was thus sentenced to death. Taken out of the town, across the river and up a hill overlooking Verulamium he prepared to die. The legionary who had been instructed to execute him could not bring himself to carry out the sentence and chose to die alongside him. Another soldier was hastily brought and Alban's head was cut off, although according to later medieval legend divine retribution soon fell upon the executioner when his eyes suddenly fell out of their sockets!

THE TEMPLE OF MITHRAS

Queen Victoria Street, London

The Persian God of Light

Every day thousands people making their way to and from work in the City of London pass by a nondescript set of steps that appear to lead up to an equally dull modern office building. Some of them might glance upwards at a pile of old stones that seem to be laid out in the manner of a ruined chapel, but few of them take the time to explore further and so do not realize that on an ugly concrete platform, just a stone's throw away from St Paul's Cathedral, there stands a relic of the very first City of London. The relic is a mysterious temple where followers of what was one of the most popular cults in the Roman Empire came to worship.

Discovered quite by accident in the aftermath of the Second World War, during building work due to bomb damage at nearby Walbrook, this temple to the Persian god of light and the sun was moved to its present site in Temple Court, Queen Victoria Street to enable construction to continue uninterrupted. As a result the reconstructed temple is now on an elevated platform some six feet above street level and thus much of the mysticism it would have possessed when it was largely a subterranean place of worship has undoubtedly been lost. Yet the way it has been put back together enables us to gain a remarkable insight into the rights and rituals of the cult of Mithras. It clearly shows us how the cult had a definite influence on the development of Christianity, the religion whose ascendancy would ultimately eclipse and obliterate Mithraism.

The Roman legions first came across the cult of Mithras in Persia (modern-day Iran) during the reign of the emperor Nero. It was one of many religious cults that the Romans brought back from the East, and initially it appealed to slaves and freedmen. However, the cult's emphasis on truth, honour and courage, coupled with its demand for discipline soon made its central deity a popular god with soldiers and traders.

ABOVE: *London's Temple of Mithras commemorates the Persian God whose cult the Romans spread throughout their Empire.*

The basic tenet of Mithraic belief was that Mithras had been born from a rock, and that his early life was one of extreme hardship and ordeal. Eventually, he was forced to pit his wits against the primordial bull, and having dragged the struggling creature to a cave, he slew it. In so doing he released its life-force for the benefit of humankind. All valuable plants and herbs grew from its body, from its blood came forth the vine, whilst its semen was the source of all useful animals.

In an attempt to re-create the surroundings of the cave where the slaying of the bull took place, Mithraic temples were always built either partially or totally underground. Worshippers were divided into seven grades, each of them marking a stage of knowledge in the cult's mysteries. An initiate started as Corax (the Raven), then progressed through the stages of Nymphus (bridegroom), Miles (soldier), Leo (lion), Perses (Persian), Heliodromus (Runner of the Sun), before reaching the ultimate grade of Pater (Father). Each rank was denoted by a specific costume and head mask exclusive to that particular grade, and initiation into the various degrees was by way of a series of demanding tests of stamina and courage.

The scores made in the stone by the continual opening of the temple doors to admit worshippers are still evident in this London Temple, as is the nave which led to an apse or altar, traces of which are still visible at the north end of the temple. Followers would have sat on benches on either side of this nave and the bases of the columns between which followers would sit can also still be seen.

Because the slaying of the bull was an integral part of the religion's foundation, sacrifices were a common part of Mithraic worship, as were shared meals of bread and wine, particularly around the festival that celebrated Mithras's springing from the rock, traditionally held on 25th December. However, when in AD 312 Constantine the Great made Christianity the official religion of the Roman Empire, Mithraism was seen as a major rival. Consequently, pagan temples began to be stamped out and the one in London appears to have been hastily abandoned at some stage in the 4th century. But early Christianity was not above borrowing certain useful elements of the religion it was attempting to quash, and the design of Mithraic temples, such as the one now stranded above the streets of modern London, became the blueprint on which Christian chapels were later based.

THE PRIORY CHURCH OF ST BARTHOLOMEW THE GREAT
SMITHFIELD, LONDON
Founded on a Vision

The Priory Church of St Bartholomew the Great is the oldest parish church in London. It possesses a dark and mysterious interior, the ancient walls of which drip with so much atmosphere that its ambience has been described as the 'holy gloom'. It is one of those churches that, the moment you step inside, you sense that it is a sacred place. The perfect spot in which to spend a few moments, or even a few hours, in peaceful contemplation, oblivious to the bustle and rush of modern London outside. For here, in this little oasis of genuine calm, time well and truly stands still.

The beginnings of this wonderful old church are tinged with the supernatural. According to legend, it was founded in 1123 by a man named Rahere who was once a jester at the court of Henry I. In November 1120, the King's only son and heir, William, was drowned when the *White Ship* was lost in a winter storm off Calais. The court was plunged into despondency, and Rahere opted to become a monk and set off on a pilgrimage to Rome. While there he fell dangerously ill with malaria and on his deathbed vowed that if he were cured and allowed to return to his own country, he would 'erect a hospital for the restoration of poor men'.

Miraculously, Rahere's prayer was answered, and he duly set off for England. On the way he had a terrible dream in which he was seized by a fearful winged creature and taken up onto a high ledge where he was set down, teetering on the brink of a yawning chasm. Just as he was about to fall, the radiant figure of St Bartholomew appeared at his side and told Rahere that he had come to save him. In return, said the saint, 'in my name thou shalt found a church… in London, at Smedfeld [Smithfield].' Thus the church was founded, and when he died in 1145, Rahere was buried inside. Although now moved from its original location, his tomb can still be viewed to the left of the high altar.

THE TEMPLE CHURCH
THE TEMPLE, LONDON
The Soldiers of Christ

Set back from the hustle and bustle that is the daily rush of modern-day Fleet Street and the Victoria Embankment, lies a magical area of London. Walk into it from the busy main roads and you are suddenly pitched back into a more genteel age. The Temple, consisting of the two honourable societies of the Middle and Inner Temples, is the domain of bewigged and robed barristers. Walking the courtyards and passageways of the Temple, especially at night when the area is bathed in the warming glow of gaslight, is a truly magical experience. It is easy to see how little it has changed since Charles Dickens wrote of it: 'Those who pace its lanes and squares may yet hear the echoes of their footsteps on the sounding stones and read upon its gates… "Who enters here leaves noise behind."'

The Temple gets its name from the Knights Templar, the military religious order founded in 1118 with the avowed intent of protecting pilgrims on the road to Jerusalem. This was their London citadel and in 1185 they built their Round Church, which was modelled on the Holy Sepulchre in Jerusalem, and which still survives today. The Templars were well connected and soon became influential in the politics of the age. They quickly attracted grants of land and money as the younger sons of noble families flocked to enrol in their ranks. By the 13th century they were one of the most powerful religious orders in Christendom. In England the Master of the Temple was frequently called to sit in the king's Parliament, and successive monarchs, King John included, stayed at the Templars' London base. The Master of the Order was by King John's side at the signing of Magna Carta. By the early years of the 14th century the Templars were more powerful than many kings and were answerable only to the Pope himself.

OPPOSITE: *Temple Church sits amidst the tranquil oasis of one of London's Inns of Court and is said to be one of the capital's most psychically charged buildings.*

But their great wealth and power attracted the jealousy and greed of many other orders, not least the Knights Hospitallers, and eventually that of the nobility and monarchs of Europe as well. In 1306 Philip IV of France was determined to rid his territories of the Templars. At dawn on Friday, 13th October 1307 Philip made his move, and with the backing of Pope Clement V, all the Templars in France were simultaneously arrested by Philip's agents. Under torture, some Templars confessed to all manner of blasphemous and indecent acts. Many of their number were burnt at the stake and eventually in 1312 the Order of the Knights Templar was officially dissolved throughout Europe.

There are many conspiracy theories concerning the real reason for the destruction of the Order, and some of them go far beyond the obvious motive that Philip simply wanted to get his hands on its wealth. Several modern-day fringe researchers have claimed that the Templars guarded secret knowledge, linking them to the lost teachings and relics of Christ, including the Holy Grail.

In London their Round Church still stands as a proud testimony to these Soldiers of Christ. In 1324 the Templars' London estate was given to the Knights Hospitallers of St John, and some of the monastery buildings were rented to law students for accommodation. The connection with the law flourished and it is lawyers who today worship in the church.

Despite its renovation following bomb damage in the Second World War, the Temple Church is still a very special and atmospheric place. The first thing that strikes you when

you enter are the effigies of knights that lie peacefully recumbent on the floor. The hustle and bustle of the world outside seems centuries away as you stand gazing down upon them, and such is the power of the building that some people claim that it is one of the most psychically charged structures in the whole of London.

Pilgrims, Pagans and Ancient Burials

✴

When the sweet showers of April fall and shoot
Down through the drought of March to pierce the root,
Bathing every vein in liquid power
From which there springs the engendering of the flower...
Then people long to go on pilgrimages
And palmers long to seek the stranger strands
Of far-off saints, hallowed in sundry lands,
And specially, from every shire's end
In England, down to Canterbury they wend
To seek the holy blissful martyr, quick
In giving help to them when they were sick.

FROM **THE CANTERBURY TALES**
BY GEOFFREY CHAUCER (1340-1400)

SUSSEX, SURREY & KENT

The south-east corner of England, with its green fields, sleepy villages, lush woodlands, rolling downs, wide beaches, high cliffs and bracing coastline, possesses a calm tranquillity that belies its stormy past. Ancient peoples have certainly left their mark on the countryside, and places such as Kits Coty House near Maidstone, despite being hijacked by later Anglo-Saxon legends, hark back to the thousands of years of human presence in this region. The Celts, Romans, Saxons, Angles and Jutes all left their imprint upon the landscape, both physically and spiritually. Memorials such as the Long Man of Wilmington stand as testimony to the longevity of human occupation and the many different beliefs that have flourished in the region. In AD 597, a peaceful though more long-lasting invasion occurred with the arrival from Rome of St Augustine, who

PAGE 62: *Canterbury Cathedral is famous as the place where Thomas á Becket was murdered in cold blood.*

PREVIOUS PAGE: *Chanctonbury Ring is said to be created by the Devil himself.*

built the first church to stand on the site now occupied by Canterbury Cathedral. It is the rich diversity of momentous and nation-shaping events that has imbued the region with an almost fabled status in its own right. Coupled with some of England's most stunning views, it offers the intrepid seeker after things mystical, a rich profusion of picturesque scenery, fascinating history and enduring legend.

CHANCTONBURY RING
NR. WASHINGTON, WEST SUSSEX
The Devil's Merry Dance

Rising to an impressive height of 238m (783ft) and affording stunning views over the surrounding countryside, the Iron Age hill-fort of Chanctonbury Ring is a dominating landmark with a peculiar air of chilling mystery. Sadly, the hurricane that so devastated southern England in 1987 also swept away many of the beech trees that were once the hill's crowning glory, and which were planted by local landowner, Charles Goring, in 1760.

There are many legends and traditions associated with the hill, chief amongst them being the belief that the Devil had

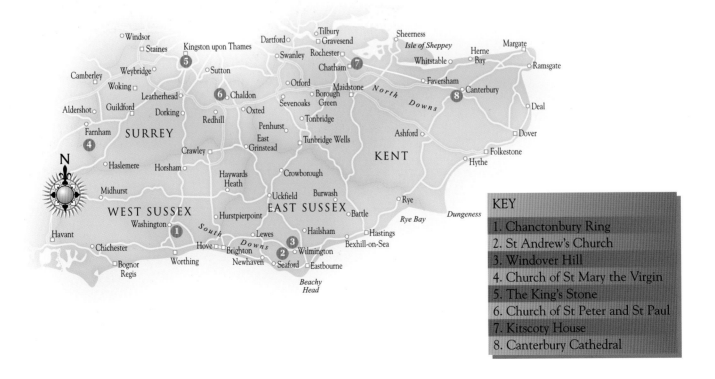

KEY
1. Chanctonbury Ring
2. St Andrew's Church
3. Windover Hill
4. Church of St Mary the Virgin
5. The King's Stone
6. Church of St Peter and St Paul
7. Kitscoty House
8. Canterbury Cathedral

a hand in its formation. He is said to have been so annoyed when he discovered that the inhabitants of Sussex were being converted to Christianity, that he endeavoured to drown them by digging a deep trench to the sea. As he dug, clods of earth flew everywhere and landed in untidy heaps across the landscape, one of which became Chanctonbury Ring. Fortunately for the residents of Sussex a wily old woman, who lived nearby, set a lighted candle upon her window ledge and placed a polished sieve behind it. This disturbed a cockerel, which began to crow loudly and the Devil, looking up from his work, mistook the candle's reflection in the sieve for the rising sun and fled without completing his task. A vestige of its supposed satanic origins is the widely held belief that if you run seven times around the summit in an anti-clockwise direction on either a dark and moonless night, or during the time it takes the clock to strike midnight, then the Devil will appear and offer you a bowl of milk, soup or porridge. Should you accept, he will either claim your soul, or else grant you your dearest wish.

ST ANDREW'S CHURCH
ALFRISTON, SUSSEX
The Cathedral of the South Downs

The beautiful 14th-century church of St Andrew's stands in a curve on the River Cuckmere, and such are its lofty proportions that it is known as 'The Cathedral of the South Downs'. Built in the shape of a Greek Cross, it has a central tower surmounted by a shingled spire and probably stands on an ancient sacred site. Indeed, according to local folklore the site on which the church stands was actually chosen by

ABOVE: *Legends abound concerning the Devil's activities at locations such as Chanctonbury Ring in West Sussex, testimony to the Church's efforts to demonize the gods of the older religion.*

supernatural forces. It seems that the church was originally intended to stand elsewhere, but each morning the builders would find that their work had been mysteriously destroyed during the night. Furthermore, the stones that they had

painstakingly laid the previous day would always end up cast over onto the mound a little way away from their building site. Realizing that someone or something might be trying to tell them something, they debated long and hard as to whether they should relocate. Their main bone of contention was that they couldn't agree on whether the nocturnal moving of the stones was the work of the Devil or of God. Then one morning a group of 'wise men' noticed four oxen lying on the mound, their bodies forming the shape of the Greek Cross, and this was taken as a sign from God that the site should indeed be moved. Thus it was that the lovely old church came to stand on a site that had, evidently, long been deemed hallowed ground.

THE LONG MAN, WINDOVER HILL
NR. WILMINGTON, EAST SUSSEX
The Silent Guardian of a Mysterious Landscape

Few sites in England are more prominent or eye-catching than this remarkable colossus, etched into the green turf of a sleepy Sussex hillside. He measures an impressive 71.5m (235ft) across by 70m (231ft) tall and his origins are shrouded in the mists of time, as thick as any fog that comes rolling across the South Downs. There are those who say that he is of prehistoric origin, others that he is Roman. Some attribute him to

LEFT: *This hefty stone that gave its name to Kingston in Surrey was where seven Anglo Saxon Kings were crowned.*

idle monks, whiling away halcyon summer afternoons in the 11th or 12th centuries. There is even evidence to suggest that he is nothing more than an 18th-century folly. He acquired his present appearance in 1874, when the site's then owner, the Duke of Devonshire, had him outlined in brick. It is still rumoured that the prudish Victorians used the opportunity of this makeover to rob him of his manhood!

The hillside on which he stands is pocked with indentations left by ancient flint mines, which local tradition has long considered proof that behind the genesis of the Long Man there lies a fearful legend of battling giants. The titans, so it is believed, lived respectively on Windover Hill and nearby Firle Beacon. One day the two quarrelled and, in their rage, began hurling massive boulders at each other. As the rocks thundered into the hillside, they are said to have left behind the indentations that can still be seen today. Eventually, the Firle giant proved victorious and his opponent fell dead onto Windover Hill, where the mighty figure of the Long Man marks the site of his grave. Is it possible that, at the root of this colourful tale, there lies a vague folk memory of an actual battle between two heroes, one of whom was buried in the vicinity?

BELOW: *Inside the church of St Peter and St Paul in Chaldon you will find a medieval wall painting that serves as a timely reminder of the rewards of sin.*

The truth is, we will probably never know to what age the Long Man actually belongs or even what purpose he originally served. He has the tantalizing ability of being all things to all people, residing as much in our imaginations as on his tranquil hillside. When we are long gone, he will still be there, a potent and timeless enigma, gazing out across a landscape he has watched over for centuries and to whose secrets and memories he will remain a silent guardian.

THE CHURCH OF ST MARY THE VIRGIN, FRENSHAM
SURREY
Stolen From the Fairy Folk

Inside the 14th-century church is an immense cauldron, which in former times may well have been used to hold the vast quantities of ale required to slake the thirsts of parishioners at village feasts. John Aubrey (1626–1697) in his *Natural History and Antiquities of the County of Surrey* records a far more colourful tradition behind the cauldron's origins. According to Aubrey, there was once a stone on Borough-hill 'in the parish of Frensham' upon which anyone could knock, declare aloud an item they wished to borrow, then leave. When they returned a disembodied voice would inform them when to collect the desired article. However, the Frensham Cauldron, so he records, 'was borrow'd here after the manner aforesaid, but not return'd according to the

promise; and though the caldron was afterwards carried to the stone it could not be receive'd, and ever since that time no borrowing there.'

THE KINGS STONE,
KINGSTON, SURREY
Where Ancient Kings were Crowned

Kingston upon Thames is the oldest of the four Royal Boroughs in England and Wales. Its name comes from the fact that seven Anglo-Saxon kings were crowned there and the stone used in their coronation ceremonies is still on view, and a silver penny from the reign of each Saxon king is set into its plinth. The last king crowned here was Ethelred II in AD 979 .

The Stone may have originally been located in the Saxon Chapel of St Mary, which used to adjoin All Saints Parish Church. When this chapel collapsed in 1730, the stone was moved to the market-place, where it was used as a mounting block by horsemen. In 1850 its true worth was recognized and it was set on a special base and placed to the south of the market, with the names of the seven kings crowned over it – Edward the Elder, Athelstan, Edmund, Edred, Edwy, Edward the Martyr and Ethelred – carved around the base. It was moved to its present position when the Guildhall was built in 1935, and now it sits forlornly, ignored by most who pass it, a forgotten relic of past grandeur and glory.

BELOW: *The huge and brightly-coloured wall painting within Chaldon Church depicts scenes from both the Old and New Testaments.*

THE CHURCH OF ST PETER AND ST PAUL
CHALDON, SURREY
The Ladder of Salvation

Just a stone's throw from the urban spread of Greater London lies the peaceful village of Chaldon. In the 19th century, workmen who were carrying out restoration on the 11th-century parish church of St Peter and St Paul made a remarkable discovery. As the vicar, the Reverend H. Shepherd, kept a watchful eye on the proceedings he happened to catch sight of 'some colour peeping out [from] beneath the whitewash'. He alerted the men who were busily removing the whitewash, and as a result of his vigilance and their carefulness, a 12th-century masterpiece was slowly uncovered. The amazing wall painting that gradually came to light has since been acknowledged as 'archaeologically at least...the most valuable and interesting wall painting in England'. It covers the whole of the church's west wall, measuring a remarkable 5.25m (17ft 3in) by 3.4m (11ft 2in), and depicts the Ladder of Salvation of the human soul, with graphic portrayals of heaven, hell and purgatory.

The remarkable picture in red, white and yellow, was probably painted by an itinerant artist-monk, and was intended as a visual aid to religious teachings. As such, it provides us with a vivid insight into the minds and beliefs of medieval worshippers. It goes a long way towards explaining why they were so willing to undertake tedious and even dangerous pilgrimages, which offered them little physical comfort, but, hopefully, gave them the chance of spiritual salvation.

The mural is in the form of a cross on which the vertical ladder and the horizontal cloud that separates heaven and hell divides the painting into four quarters. The lower right quarter shows the tree of knowledge in the Garden of Eden. The serpent that witnessed Adam's fall hides in its branches, representing the beginning of all human sin. To its left two demons hold aloft a bridge of spikes, across which dishonest tradesmen must make their way. The first to cross is the blacksmith making a horseshoe without an anvil. He is followed by a mason without a chisel, a spinner without a distaff, and a potter

OPPOSITE: *The Church of St Mary the Virgin in Frensham boasts a cauldron that was reputedly borrowed from the fairies.*

without a wheel. An eyeless usurer is already in the flames beneath the bridge. A fat purse of money hangs from his neck, and three bags of gold hang from his waist. He is being forced to eat red hot coins by two demons who jab him in the head with their forks to make him eat faster. To his right are two figures that depict envy, while the two figures to his left are being encouraged by demons to embrace each other – they represent lust. The remaining deadly sins are scattered around in small scenes with human figures, to the left of the ladder.

In the bottom left quarter another demon is busily pulling souls off the ladder of salvation, or impaling them on the prongs of his fork. A ferocious fire rages across the panel and heats a huge cauldron that is crammed with suffering souls who two more demons are jabbing with their pitchforks. The one to the left holds a group of souls above a demonic wolf who snaps at their feet, suggesting that they were probably intended to represent dancers, who were especially denounced by the monks of that age. To the right of the cauldron a dog is shown preparing to bite a lady's hand, and probably alludes to a wealthy woman who pampered her dogs and treated them to rich nibbles that she should have given to the poor.

The top half of the mural provides welcome relief from the horrendous torments so graphically portrayed in the bottom section. On the far right, Jesus is shown thrusting the staff of his banner into the mouth of a bound Satan, as Adam, Eve and others fly free. A wavy edge containing the head and shoulders of Christ, surrounded by an aureole with the sun on his right and the moon on his left, is shown above the ladder, on the top rungs of which the souls who have now reached heaven find their ascent far more graceful and much less traumatic as two angels help them into paradise.

Finally, to the left of the ladder the Archangel Michael holds the scales for the weighing of the souls, while another angel is carrying a tablet on which are recorded good deeds. Satan, with his slavering tongue poked out, has roped together a group of souls who are too light in virtue, while slyly trying to push down the scales on his side and thus secure another victim.

This extraordinary picture is testimony to the unshakable belief in a very vivid and real afterlife that the people of England held 700 years ago. Even today, standing and gazing upon the remarkable figures on the walls of this magnificent church, you can feel definite pangs of guilt course through your veins, and you come away resolute in your belief that a change of lifestyle might be to your definite advantage.

LEFT: *Despite its neglected appearance and the unsightly fence that surrounds it Kits Coty House still manages to summon up an aura of mystery.*

KITS COTY HOUSE
Nr. Chatham, Kent
Catigern's Possible Resting Place

Despite efforts to make this impressive Neolithic chambered tomb look as unattractive as possible by caging it behind an ugly iron fence, Kits Coty House has shown itself able to shrug off the shackles of its imprisonment and manages to exude a mystical aura that transcends the centuries. Some people simply refer to it as Kits Coty, since *coty* actually means 'house'. But few who undertake the squelching plod along the muddy path that leads to it can fail to be moved by both its location and its evident antiquity. Legend tells that the Kit of its name refers to Catigern, one of the sons of Vortigern, who with his brother Vortimer fought Hengist and his sibling Horsa here, around 455 AD. A battle that is recorded both in the *Historia Brittonum* and *Anglo-Saxon Chronicle*. 'He [Vortigern] had three sons,' says chapter 44 of the *Historia Brittonum*, 'the eldest was Vortimer, who, as we have seen, fought four times against the Saxons, and put them to flight; the second Categirn, who was slain in the same battle with Horsa…' We don't actually know who won the battle, but following his death Catigern was supposedly buried at what is now known as Kits Coty House.

The stones themselves, which consist of three hefty upright stones, surmounted by a fourth large one, are all that have survived from the chamber of the long barrow, and have been dated to between 4300 to 3000 BC. When Samuel Pepys, the diarist, visited the site in the 17th century he described finding, 'Three great stones standing upright and a great round one lying on them, of great bigness, although not so big as those on Salisbury Plain. But certainly it is a thing of great antiquity and I am mightily glad to have seen it.' A large stone, known as the 'General's Stone', once stood at the west end of the long barrow, but this was blown up in 1867, probably to make it easier to plough the land.

Kits Coty has withstood the ravages of both nature and time and sits forlornly in its remote field. An aura of sadness seems to radiate from the stones themselves, yet no one who comes to this site of ancient mystery can fail to be moved by the atmosphere of timelessness. This coupled with the lovely views over the Medway Valley makes for a spiritually refreshing yet historically fascinating visit.

CANTERBURY CATHEDRAL
Kent
Angels not Angles

In the spring of AD 597 St Augustine landed in England with instructions from Pope Gregory the Great to convert its inhabitants to Christianity. As a deacon in Rome, Gregory had been much taken with a group of fair-haired slaves he had seen for sale in the market-place. When he asked their nationality he was told that they were Angles, to which he made the famous punning riposte that they were 'not Angles but Angels'. The story is probably apocryphal and its veracity is difficult to ascertain today, but certainly something persuaded Gregory that the Angles were worth converting to Christianity. As pope he persuaded St Augustine and a band of fellow monks to set sail as missionaries. So it was that Augustine arrived in Kent and set about his duty of bringing the Good News of Christ to its pagan people.

The missionaries were received with courtesy by Ethelbert of Kent, a pagan king who was married to a Christian wife. Ethelbert agreed to grant Augustine an audience and so the two men met at Thanet, with the King seated in the open and Augustine and his fellow monks standing before him with their standards, a silver cross and a portrait of Christ placed where the King could see them. Having listened to Augustine's message, Ethelbert told the missionary that he and his people could not be expected to abandon the religion that they had always followed, but he granted permission for the monks to go to Canterbury and preach their message to anyone who would listen.

Eventually, however, Ethelbert did find himself moved by Augustine's message and on the following Whit Sunday, he was baptized at Canterbury and within a few years most of his subjects had followed suit. Thus began the conversion of England to the Christian religion, as gradually its message spread throughout the other Anglo-Saxon kingdoms. Augustine was made Archbishop of the English and established his See at Canterbury, where he founded a monastery. From this foundation eventually grew Christ Church Cathedral, which today is an awe-inspiring mix of Romanesque and Perpendicular Gothic architecture.

At a little after 4 p.m. on 29th December 1170, four Norman knights murdered the then Archbishop of Canterbury, Thomas á Becket. They were acting upon the outburst made by King Henry II: 'What Miserable drones and traitors have I nourished… who allow their lord to be treated with such shameful contempt by a low-born cleric.' By this brutal act they sparked off one of the greatest saint-hero cults of the Middle Ages, and turned the unappealingly arrogant, haughty and self-centred Becket into a posthumous international icon. Within three years the dead archbishop had been canonized and the shrine of St Thomas at Canterbury soon became one of the Christian world's greatest places of pilgrimage, and countless miracles were said to have taken place there.

OPPOSITE: *Canterbury Cathedral was where Thomas á Becket was murdered by four knights acting on an outburst of King Henry II. His death made the Cathedral the centre of one of medieval England's greatest saint-hero cults.*

Toppled Abbeys and Soaring Glories

BUT PEACEFUL WAS THE NIGHT
WHEREIN THE PRINCE OF LIGHT
HIS RAIGN OF PEACE UPON THE EARTH BEGAN:
THE WINDES WITH WONDER WHIST,
SMOOOTHLY THE WATERS KIST,
WHISPERING NEW JOYS TO THE MILDE OCEAN,
WHO NOW HAVE QUITE FORGOT TO RAVE,
WILE BIRDS OF CALM SIT BROODING ON THE CHARMED WAVE.

FROM 'HYMN ON THE MORNING OF CHRIST'S NATIVITY'
BY JOHN MILTON (1608-1674).

CAMBRIDGESHIRE, NORFOLK, SUFFOLK & ESSEX

The eastern counties of England occupy the region that once formed the ancient kingdom of East Anglia, whose inhabitants consisted of the North Folk (Norfolk) and the South Folk (Suffolk). Bounded to the west by the swamps of the Fens, buffered to the east and north by

PREVIOUS PAGE & 74: *Norwich Cathedral is a beautiful building that is home to several amusing, but definitely less attractive, Green Men.*

the sea, and hemmed in to the south by the thick woodlands of Saxon Essex, it was for centuries an aloof and mysterious region, populated by a hardy and resourceful people. This was always a region where mysticism and spirituality held sway. It is the area that is home to one of the oldest churches in England, at Bradwell in Essex. It is where one of the holiest shrines of medieval Britian was situated at Walsingham in Norfolk. The region also has a more sinister aspect to its history, for it is a sad fact that during the

KEY

1. Ely Cathedral
2. Our Lady of Walsingham
3. Norwich Cathedral
4. The Abbey Ruins
5. Sutton Hoo
6. Waltham Abbey
7. St Peter's on the Wall

witchcraft hysteria of the 16th and 17th centuries more people were executed in East Anglia than in any other part of the country. This was partly as a result of the Puritan stranglehold on the region, which had outlawed holy water and abolished exorcism, leaving the God-fearing people of the area defenceless against the Devil and sundry other evil spirits that they still believed in. All in all this is an area of sharp contrasts and it is these that make it a truly fascinating region to explore.

ELY CATHEDRAL
CAMBRIDGESHIRE
The Lantern of the Fens

In AD 637 the East Anglian Princess Ethelreda decided to leave her second husband, the King of Northumbria, and become a nun. She made her way to her principality of the Isle of Ely and there founded a convent of which she became abbess. Her original foundation was destroyed by the Danes, and when it was restored in 970 it became a Benedictine monastery and its cathedral became a great favourite with the Anglo-Saxon kings.

Following the Norman Conquest of 1066, Simeon, a kinsman of William the Conqueror, was appointed Abbot of Ely, and in 1083 he set about rebuilding the Saxon cathedral. The majestic structure that rose on the Island of Ely is now acknowledged as one of the best examples of Romanesque architecture in England. It dominates the surrounding low-lying countryside and the fact that it is visible from miles around, sometimes appearing to float on the early morning mists, has led to it being dubbed 'the ship of the Fens'.

The appearance of the present-day cathedral owes a lot to a potentially tragic event that occurred in the 14th century. On 22nd February 1322, just as the monks were retiring to their cells, the Norman tower of the cathedral collapsed into the choir 'with such a shock,' recounted a chronicler, 'that it was thought an earthquake had taken place.' Luckily, no one was killed and we are told that the sacrist, Alan de Walsingham, 'rose up by night and came and stood over the heap of ruins not knowing whither to turn. But recovering his courage, and confident in the help of God and of His kind Mother Mary,

RIGHT: *The soaring grandeur of Ely Cathedral is the perfect place to crane your neck in order to absorb the centuries of spirituality that surround you.*

and in the merits of the holy virgin, Ethelreda, he set his hand to the work.' It took six years to complete the central octagon tower, and a further 14 to construct the wooden lantern tower that surmounts it. But what Alan de Walsingham created is without doubt the cathedral's most striking feature, a uniquely splendid structure that is a visual work of genius, and a masterpiece of medieval engineering that seems to somehow float magically above the central crossing of Ely Cathedral.

In addition to this magnificent tower, Ely can also boast the largest Lady Chapel in England, this, too, being the work of the designing genius of Alan de Walsingham. It doesn't take much imagination to picture what it must have been like in medieval times when it would have been richly decorated. Indeed, the overall effect would have been spectacular – a true celebration of the glory of God and an inspiration for pious wonder. However, during the Dissolution of the Monasteries (1536–1540) under Henry VIII, who strove to establish himself as head of the Church in England, the rich furnishings and statuary were either defaced or destroyed. Now it is only possible to catch occasional glimpses of the former splendour. However, several magnificent features did manage to survive the state-sponsored vandalism, among them the wonderfully ornate Prior's Door, which once led into the cloisters, and which can boast a rich array of fabulous Norman carvings around its archway.

Ely Cathedral stands as a testimony to the sheer determination and vision of its creators. It is a place in which to stand with your head held high and your neck craned in order that you might take in the centuries of history and spirituality that surround you, as you glory at the sheer force of the faith of those who raised this magnificent building. As you gaze upon its soaring walls, perhaps gasping at the impressive majesty of its lantern tower, you cannot help but feel that this is a powerful and moving expression of the human spirit.

OPPOSITE: *Our Lady of Walsingham sprang from a long ago vision and became a shrine of such colossal importance that it was known as 'England's Nazareth.'*

ABOVE: *Norwich Cathedral boasts a particularly fine specimen of that most enigmatic of English folk symbols, a so-called Green Man.*

OUR LADY OF WALSINGHAM
WALSINGHAM, NORFOLK
A Holy Shrine Founded on a Vision

The ruins of an Augustinian priory church recall the days before the Dissolution of the Monasteries (1536–1540) when Walsingham was one of Europe's major destinations for pilgrimage. Its origins are said to date back to 1061 when Richeldis de Faverches – wife of the Lord of the Manor of Walsingham, and a woman known for her religious devotion – had a vision in which the Virgin Mary appeared to her and took her in spirit to the house in Nazareth where the Angel Gabriel had announced the news of Jesus' birth. Gabriel asked her to build a replica of it in Walsingham. According to legend the house was miraculously constructed while Richeldis held a prayer vigil. The house became the shrine of Our Lady of Walsingham and in 1150 her son, Geoffrey de Faverches, arranged for the Augustinan canons to build a priory next to the 'Holy House'.

The shrine, which became known as 'England's Nazareth', flourished, and in 1226 received the first of many royal visits when Henry III stopped by. Edward II, Edward III, Henry IV and Henry VII all followed in his footsteps and in so doing helped the shrine to grow in both popularity and wealth. The Dutch scholar Erasmus visited the shrine in 1513 and left a tantalizing description of what he saw. 'When you look in you would say it is the abode of saints, so brilliantly does it shine on all sides with gems, gold and silver… Our Lady stands in the dark at the right side of the altar… a little image, remarkable neither for its size, material or workmanship.'

Later, Henry VIII stayed at Barsham Manor and walked two miles barefoot to Walsingham, where he placed a 'gold circlet round Our Lady's neck'. However, this humble act of piety did not prevent him setting his covetous gaze upon the monastery's wealth, and despite the fact that Walsingham had been one of the first religious houses to sign the Oath of Supremacy, accepting Henry as head of the Church in England, the King gave orders in April 1537 that all the wealth of the religious shrine at Walsingham was to be removed. A group of 11 local men, including Nicholas Myleham, the canon of Walsingham, were subsequently hanged, beheaded and quartered for objecting to the despoilment. In 1538 the statue of the Virgin Mary was taken to London and burnt. The shrine and priory church were both destroyed, and Walsingham's days of glory and pilgrimage were over.

Interest was revived in 1897 when Pope Leo XIII re-founded the Ancient Shrine of Our Lady of Walsingham and the first pre-Reformation pilgrimage took place to the only building that had survived the Dissolution, the 14th-century Slipper Chapel. In 1921 the Reverend Alfred Hope-Patten was appointed Vicar of Walsingham, and was he who had the idea of basing a new statue of Our Lady of Walsingham on the image that was on the seal of the medieval priory. The following year the new statue was set up in the Parish Church of St Mary, and in 1931 it was moved to a newly constructed 'Holy House'.

In 1938 a church was built over the Holy House, and today this forms the shrine of Our Lady of Walsingham. In the years that followed, a complex of buildings sprouted around the site and these now cater to the needs of the large number of pilgrims who flock to the shrine to absorb its spirituality.

The shrine is also dedicated to the bringing closer of the various branches of the Christian religion. The Slipper Chapel is now a centre of Roman Catholic worship. There is also an Anglican shrine, an 18th-century Methodist chapel and a Russian Orthodox church. Whether you are a devout believer or just a curious visitor you cannot fail to be moved by the air of tranquillity and peace with which the whole complex seems to be imbued. It is a wonderful place to while away a few precious hours, and has the ability to recharge the batteries and fire the imagination of even the most jaded amongst us.

NORWICH CATHEDRAL
NORFOLK
The Green Man or Foliate Head
Norwich Cathedral is a place of rare beauty that offers visitors an impressive collection of that most enigmatic of English folklore heroes, the Green Man. These foliate heads (the term Green Man is actually a 20th-century invention first used by Lady Raglan in 1939 in an article she wrote for *Folk-Lore*) are decorative images often found in churches from the Norman and Gothic periods. They often show male heads with leafy sprays either sprouting from the mouth, eyes and ears, or else covering the face so that it peers out from behind a thick bush of greenery. They are found on corbels, capitals, roof bosses, choir stalls, misericords and chancel screens, in fact just about anywhere that required some form of embellishment. What is interesting is that the craftsmen who created them employed a rich array of secular and humorous themes.

RIGHT: *The passage of time has left the once proud arches of Bury St Edmund's Abbey tottering in ruin.*

The foliate heads arrived in England in the 12th century. Their origins probably lay in the late Roman art leaf-masks that depicted deities and supernatural creatures and beings. They became very popular with Gothic craftsmen since they combined two of the preferred images of medieval artists, that of lush flora and the human face. The various moods and expressions with which foliate heads are adorned are as varied as the locations in which they are found. Some have

a tranquil, almost resigned look. Others are gloomy or angry. Some have a threatening or mocking feel about them, while others stick out their tongues as if blowing a long and sustained raspberry at passers-by and the world in general.

As for their original purpose and true meaning, this is far more difficult to ascertain, and many theories have been put forward. Some believe that the so-called Green Man was an ancient device used by the early Christian Church as a symbol of the resurrection of Christ. The theologian Rabanus Maurus (784–856) had written, admittedly before their introduction into England, that the leafy sprays were intended to represent lusts of the flesh, and that the figures as a whole symbolized depraved men bound for eternal damnation. Some 20th-century writers have come to see them as Christian adaptations of pagan symbols, which were allowed to exist side by side with other more

conventional Christian devices in an attempt to absorb but ultimately stamp out cherished and long-held beliefs among local communities.

Of course we will never know for sure why medieval craftsmen devoted their energies to creating these enigmatic symbols on the walls and roofs of churches. It may have simply been a decorative device to add colour to structures that were intended to celebrate God and the world he created. Today, we are used to thinking of churches as being sombre and unadorned places, but in the Middle Ages they would have been bright and cheerful, and their walls and ceilings would have been adorned with an abundance of rich decoration in vivid colours such as gold and green. Perhaps these foliate heads were intended as embellishments to those artworks. Could they have also been intended to remind worshippers of their ultimate fate, that of burial in the cold earth from which greenery and plant life springs?

These heads are a tantalizing enigma from the past, but what is certain is that the craftsmen who created them possessed both humour and skill.

THE ABBEY RUINS
BURY ST EDMUND'S, SUFFOLK
The Watchful Wolf

St Edmund was a king of East Anglia who was gruesomely murdered by a raiding party of Vikings in AD 870. According to an account of the saint's life, written a little over a hundred years after his slaying:

> … *the heathen were madly angry because of his faith, because he called upon Christ to help him. They shot at him with javelins as if for their amusement, until he was all beset with their shots… When Hingwar, the wicked seaman, saw that the noble king would not deny Christ, but with steadfast faith ever called upon Him, he commanded men to behead him, and the heathen did so. For while he was yet calling upon Christ, the heathen drew away the saint to slay him, and struck off his head with a single blow, and his soul departed joyfully to Christ. There was a certain man at hand, whom God was hiding from the heathen, who heard all this and told it afterward just as we tell it here.*

The account goes on to tell how, after the Vikings had departed, Edmund's followers returned to find his headless corpse, and were most upset that they could not find his head. For three days they searched until a ghostly voice called them to a bramble thicket where a grey wolf was standing guard over the missing head. The wolf escorted the relic to the nearby town, and then turned back to its wood, leaving the King's followers to hastily bury their sovereign and build a rough church over the spot where he lay.

Many years after the martyrdom, the remains were transferred to the abbey at Bedricsworth. When Edmund's remains were exhumed, those present were astonished to find that the head and body had fused back together, and the wounds inflicted by the Vikings had been miraculously healed, so that the saintly king looked as uncorrupted as he had been in life. As a result the abbey became a major centre of pilgrimage, and people journeyed from far and wide to seek the aid and intercession of the martyr-king, and within decades it became known by a new name, the name it has today, Burgh or Bury St Edmunds.

Following the Norman invasion, the abbey flourished and eventually became one of the largest Benedictine monasteries in England. Life for the monks, however, was not all contemplation and meditation, for from the 14th century onwards they encountered increasing hostility from the local people who grew tired of being under the influence of this powerful abbey. They had barely recovered from the financial burden of rebuilding, when in 1431, the west tower of the abbey church suddenly collapsed. Their coffers were stretched even further two years later when Henry VI arrived to spend Christmas with the monks, and so enjoyed their hospitality that he stayed for four months. Finally, in 1465 the entire church was destroyed by fire and the disasters that had beset the monastery over the previous centuries appear to have been brought to an end. The abbey of Bury St Edmund's was rebuilt and enjoyed a relatively trouble-free existence until its destruction in 1539 during the Dissolution of the Monasteries. It was stripped of all its valuable materials and artefacts, and the ruins became a useful source of stone for local builders.

Today, the passage of time has left the once proud arches of what must have been a magnificent abbey, mouldering in decay. Its haunting buttresses have tottered and fallen. Its stark stone columns now loom over eerie crumbling walls, while empty windows look mournfully down on the shattered cloisters and aisles where monastic feet once shuffled in peaceful contemplation. Yet the ruins have a strange enchantment about them and to walk amongst them, or to stand silently by the old gatehouse, is to absorb the energy of what many acknowledge as being one of the most spiritually charged locations in England.

SUTTON HOO
NR. WOODBRIDGE, SUFFOLK
He Sailed into Eternity

'*They laid then the beloved chieftain, giver of rings, on the ship's bosom, glorious by the mast. There were brought many treasures, ornaments from far-off lands. Never have I heard that a vessel was more fairly fitted-out with war-weapons and battle-raiment, swords and coats of mail. On his bosom lay a host of treasures, where were to travel far with him into the power of the flood.*'

On 25th July 1939, archaeologists began excavating a series of circular mounds on the property of Mrs E. M. Pretty at Sutton Hoo. Several of the burial mounds had already been explored the previous year, but it was discovered that they had been plundered long before, and anything of true note or value had been carried away. However, the few artefacts and iron rivets that the archaeologists did uncover had proved intriguing, and they looked forward to being able to return the next summer. As they began their fresh dig in 1939 they were, no doubt, expecting to make more interesting finds but nothing could have prepared them for what they were about to uncover as they dug into the largest of the mounds. Digging carefully into its depths they were amazed to discover the detailed impression of a large ship which, it was soon realized, may well have been the final resting place of an Anglo-Saxon king. Although nothing actually remained of the main body of the ship itself, save for the clear impression of the hull in the earth, together with hundreds of rivets marking the plank runs, the dimensions of the impression showed that it had been almost 27m (90ft) long and 4.5m (15ft) wide, and that it had room to accommodate 20 rowers on each side. The inestimable historical value of the artefacts and treasures that were also discovered, and the insight they give us into the culture, beliefs and sophistication of our Anglo-Saxon forbears, has led to this remarkable site being hailed as nothing less than 'page one of English History'.

Both pagan and Christian symbols were present amongst the wonderful treasures that came to light. The objects were clearly the chattels of a warrior-king, and included his helmet and coat of mail, sword and shield, spears and axe-hammer, together with a magnificent gold-and-garnet purse lid, decorated with animal and abstract designs, inside which

ABOVE: *The glorious treasures that were uncovered inside the magnificent burial mound at Sutton Hoo are amongst the finest artefacts and treasures to survive from the days of the Anglo-Saxons.*

were found 37 small Merovingian (Gaulish) gold coins dating from the 620s. In total 41 items of solid gold were discovered (all of them are now on display in the British Museum). Even the more mundane, everyday objects proved enthralling and included buckets, tubs and cauldrons, a collection of silver bowls from the eastern Mediterranean, wooden cups, bottles and a pair of large drinking horns, all with silver-gilt fittings. Evidently, the warrior-king was to want for nothing on his voyage into the afterlife.

Yet, despite the glimmer of light that the items discovered throw onto the Dark Ages, it is still not known for certain who was buried here, if anyone at all. Since no human remains have ever been discovered at the site it has been surmised that the burial may well have been a 'symbolic' one for a king who was lost at sea, or who died in battle. Others have suggested that since the remains of a coffin were uncovered then the body was in fact interred in the ship, but due to the acidity of the soil all traces of it have long since vanished.

If, indeed, the remains of a king did lie at rest on the boat, then a likely contender was Redwald, a Saxon *bretwalda*, or king, of East Anglia. According to the Venerable Bede (*c.*673–735) in his *Ecclesiastical History of the English People*, Redwald ruled East Anglia in 616. He was partially converted to Christianity at the Kentish court of King Ethelbert, but on his return to East Anglia his wife persuaded him back into his heathen faith. It seems that Redwald was happy to honour both heathen gods and the Christian God, and he constructed a Christian altar alongside the pagan one at his temple. The combination of Christian and heathen symbols found in the Sutton Hoo ship burial certainly suggest an occupant who was ostensibly heathen but was also influenced by Christianity.

In recent years further excavations of seven more mounds have led to other interesting finds. One contained two

graves, that of an Anglo-Saxon warrior in a coffin buried with a bridal and a harness, and alongside him was the grave of a horse. More gruesomely, a number of execution graves have also been revealed. Dating from the 7th to the 11th centuries, their macabre contents included hanged, decapitated and mutilated bodies.

All in all the remarkable finds at Sutton Hoo provide us with a rare opportunity to enjoy a unique glimpse into a period of our history known as the Dark Ages. They prove beyond doubt that those who lived during this hidden period were far removed from the primitive and uncultured heathens that the era's name suggests. Sutton Hoo stands as a lasting monument to the Dark Age kings of East Anglia, while its treasures stand as a glittering testimony to the skill and sophistication of their craftsmen.

WALTHAM ABBEY
ESSEX
King Harold's Final Resting Place
Bordering the 2,400 hectares (6,000 acres) of the magnificent Epping Forest, the battered walls of Waltham Abbey rise majestically from their surroundings, and despite a ceaseless tide of urban encroachment, still manage to keep themselves aloof from the advances and intrusions of the modern age.

The story behind the founding of the monastery and town dates back to the reign of King Cnut (1017–1035), when a member of the royal court, Tovi the Proud, brought a flint cross that may have contained a fragment of the 'true cross' from his estate in Somerset to Waltham. It is from this that the old name for the district, Waltham Holy Cross, was

ABOVE: *Waltham Abbey in Essex was the both place where Harold Godwinson was cured of paralysis, and where he was finally laid to rest several years after his death at the Battle of Hastings.*

derived. Legend holds that the sacred relic was discovered on a hilltop near Glastonbury and that it was placed on a cart drawn by 12 red and 12 white oxen, the intention being to take the cross to Glastonbury Abbey. The oxen, however, appear to have had other ideas and refused to go in the direction of Glastonbury but instead made their way across country until they came to Waltham, where they stopped by the church. This was seen as a sign from God and hence Waltham became the shrine of the cross, known as the Holy Rood.

Harold Godwinson, Earl of Wessex, was said to have been cured of paralysis when he came to pray at the church and he showed his gratitude by re-founding it in 1060. By the time he ascended the throne of England as King Harold II in 1066 the church had become famed as a place of miracles, and pilgrims flocked to it. Harold, however, was killed at the Battle of Hastings (1066), and six years after his death his body was reputedly brought to Waltham Cross for reburial. Today, two stones to the east of the present church building are said to mark the spot where the last Anglo-Saxon king of England lies interred. An inscription on one reads: THIS STONE MARKS THE POSITION OF THE HIGH ALTAR BEHIND WHICH KING HAROLD IS SAID TO HAVE BEEN BURIED 1066. The other says: HAROLD KING OF ENGLAND OBVT 1066.

In 1177, as part of his atonement for the murder of Thomas á Becket, Henry II re-founded the church as a priory of Augustinian canons, and in 1183 it became an abbey. The abbey brought a great deal of prosperity to the town as pilgrims flocked to pay their respects to the 'Holy Cross'. Its proximity to London made it an ideal venue for the royal court, as kings and their courtiers would come to pray in the great abbey and enjoy the hunting in Epping Forest.

It was at Waltham Abbey that Henry VIII first met Thomas Cranmer (1489–1556) and so began the process that led to the English Reformation, part of which included the Dissolution of the Monasteries. The great abbey at Waltham managed to hold out against the King's voracious appetite for seizing church lands and estates for several years, but in March 1540 it became the last abbey in the country to succumb. The nave from the 12th-century rebuilding survived the dissolution and has continued as the parish nave to this day, part of Waltham Abbey Church. The tower at the west end of the church, which dominates the town today, dates from 1556 and was constructed from stones taken from the demolished abbey buildings. It was built at the church's west end as opposed to its east end because the church was starting to lean and was in need of support.

The abbey interior today is truly spectacular, due largely to the endeavours of William Burges. the Victorian architect and designer who undertook restoration work during the 1860–70s. Other leading Victorian artists contributed to the renovations and one of the church's chief glories is without doubt the magnificent ceiling, which was executed to Burges's design by Sir Edward Poynter. The paintings, executed on canvas, show the four elements and the 12 signs of the zodiac, together with the activities, such as ploughing and weaving, appropriate to each of the signs. They do not seem in the least bit out of place in this lofty and breath-takingly beautiful place of worship. Just to reiterate their suitability for a Christian church, a notice by the entrance informs visitors that these dazzling images are in no way connected with occultism or any other such non-Christian practice.

ST PETER'S ON THE WALL
BRADWELL, ESSEX
An Isolated Place of Ancient Sanctity

The remote chapel of St Peter's On the Wall is about as far away from the modern age as you could ever wish to be. Built in AD 654 by St Cedd from the fabric of Othona, a Roman fort, this ancient place of worship – overlooking land, sea and tidal saltings – has stood on the estuary of the River Blackwater for over 1,300 years, which makes it one of the oldest churches is Britain. It isn't grand or picturesque in the conventional sense of the word. Its beauty lies in its pure simplicity, and no one who traipses across the wilderness of wind-rattled grasses that surround it, opens the heavy door and then often struggles to force it shut against the howling wind, can fail to fall beneath its spell. The unadorned rough walls offer a peaceful haven, not only from the salt-laden gales that frequently come lashing in from the grey North Sea, but also from the pressures of the modern age. It is a very spiritual place in which it is possible to find genuine solitude as you contemplate the awesome weight of history that this magical chapel evokes.

BELOW: *Windswept and isolated, this little chapel is a wonderful place in which to connect with the spirits of nature.*

Ancient Footprints on the Sands of Time

I SAW ETERNITY THE OTHER NIGHT
LIKE A GREAT RING OF PURE AND ENDLESS LIGHT,
ALL CALM, AS IT WAS BRIGHT,
AND ROUND BENEATH IT, TIME IN HOURS, DAYS, YEARS
DRIV'N BY THE SPHERES
LIKE A VAST SHADOW MOV'D, IN WHICH THE WORLD
AND ALL HER TRAIN WERE HURL'D.

FROM 'ETERNITY'
BY HENRY VAUGHAN (1621-1695).

NOTTINGHAMSHIRE,
LINCOLNSHIRE, LEICESTERSHIRE &
NORTHAMPTONSHIRE

The counties that stretch from the Lincolnshire coast to the flat arable pastures of the East and West Midlands have, over the millennia, been home to many different peoples. Celts, Romans and Vikings have all left their mark both upon the varied landscape and the folk memory of the region. There are some genuine surprises in this part of Britain. Northamptonshire's Triangular Lodge, for example, stands as a vivid testimony to the unshakable faith of a man who was willing to risk imprisonment and persecution for what he truly believed in. Bardney Abbey provides an impressive reminder of how important relics of saints were in the world of medieval pilgrimages, while Nottinghamshire's Hemlock Stone may well have once been a place where the Druids carried out their mysterious rites and rituals.

PREVIOUS PAGE & 86: Crowland Abbey was built on a desolate island, a perfect place to 'get away from it all'.

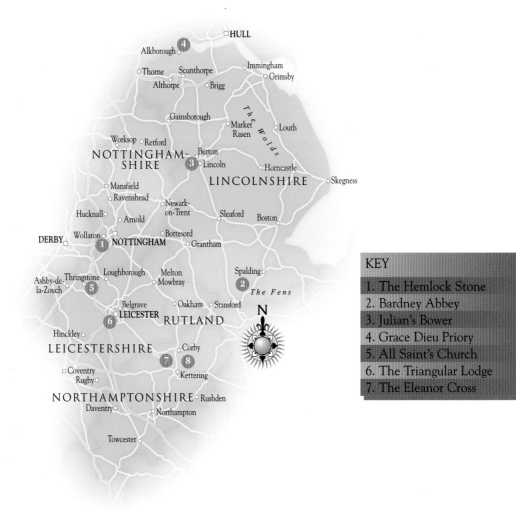

KEY

1. The Hemlock Stone
2. Bardney Abbey
3. Julian's Bower
4. Grace Dieu Priory
5. All Saint's Church
6. The Triangular Lodge
7. The Eleanor Cross

THE HEMLOCK STONE
WOLLATON, NOTTINGHAMSHIRE
Satan's Badly Aimed Missile

The Hemlock Stone is a brooding geological outcrop that sits amidst the glorious park and woodland of Stapleford Hill. Nobody knows for certain how it got its name, and there is even debate over whether its curious appearance is the work of man, through years of quarrying, or the work of nature. Inevitably, legends abound to explain how it came to be in its current position. One of the most popular concerns a monk at Lenton Priory, four miles to the west, who, finding himself plagued by insomnia, decided that the Devil must be behind his inability to sleep. He knelt down and began to pray hard that he might be released from Satan's demonic grip. So fervent were his prayers, however, that he actually woke the Devil who was sleeping on Stoney Clouds, near Sandiacre. Furious at being woken from his slumbers the Devil let out a roar of indignation, and scooping up a lump of rock, he flung it with all his might hoping to destroy both the interfering monk and his priory. But his aim fell short and the stone landed instead on Stapleford Hill where it has remained ever since. Another equally unlikely supposition is that the weird-looking stone is in fact a meteorite that crashed to earth long ago.

As varied as those of its origins are the theories as to what the stone has been used for. A popular piece of folklore suggests that witches once gathered at the site and would use the poisonous hemlock plant in their potions. Some believe that the stone may well have been used by the Druids in their rituals, and that it may have been a focal point on which fires were lit to celebrate Celtic festivals such as Beltane. There is a tradition in the area that these fires were still being lit on the stone in the early 19th century. A healing well known as the 'Sick Dyke' used to stand near to the Hemlock Stone, and several writers have suggested that this well was incorporated into rituals performed at the stone. Whatever its use, the Hemlock Stone has certainly been a local landmark for hundreds, if not thousands, of years. No doubt people from past ages and forgotten cultures have gazed upon it and may well have wondered, who placed this enigmatic lump of rock here and why?

ABOVE: *Nottinghamshire's Hemlock Stone is a curious landmark, and its origins are shrouded in mystery.*

CROWLAND ABBEY
CROWLAND, LINCOLNSHIRE
A Place to Get Away From The World

In the 7th century Crowland was an island, rising from the mist-shrouded marshes of the Fens. It was an isolated and desolate spot and its very name is derived from the Old English for 'Wild land'. Such a bleakly barren location is an ideal place to retire to if you wish to get away from the world, and so on St Bartholomew's Day AD 699 St Guthlac, a young man who had renounced the comforts of the world, came to Crowland and established a hermit's cell. Here he intended to dedicate himself to an austere life of holy contemplation.

As time passed, Guthlac's reputation for sanctity grew and he became a sought-after figure in the hope that his holiness might rub off on those who came to visit him. Amongst his supporters was Aethelbald, a claimant to the throne of the kingdom of Mercia. He was delighted when Guthlac prophesied that he would most certainly inherit the throne. Aethelbald promised that if the prophecy came to pass then he would show his appreciation by founding a monastery in Guthlac's honour. True to his word, when Aethelbald did indeed become king of Mercia he set about fulfilling his pledge, and on St Bartholomew's Day AD 716, two years after Guthlac's death, he founded Crowland Abbey.

However, over the centuries that followed the monastery was far from the peaceful place of contemplation its founder had hoped it would be. In 870 an attack by a group of rampaging Danes caught the monks unawares, and in the skirmish that followed, the abbot was killed and the buildings burnt down. Much of the abbey was restored by Abbot Turketyl in the mid-10th century, but a terrible fire in 1091 destroyed Turketyl's Saxon buildings. Again Crowland was rebuilt, this time in the Norman style, but then in 1118 much of it was destroyed by an earthquake and the rest was finished off by another in 1143. Surviving sections of that first Norman abbey can be seen in the font and the west arch of the central tower.

The abbey was rebuilt again, and enjoyed a comparatively trouble-free few centuries before its final destruction in 1539, during the Dissolution of the Monasteries in the reign of Henry VIII. The nave of the abbey church and two side aisles were left standing and were used as the parish church for Crowland, but only the north aisle now remains. However, enough of the abbey has survived to give an impression of what a glorious place it must once have been. Above the west door are quatrefoil carvings that show scenes from the life of Guthlac, and statues that depict other saints connected to the abbey. As

OPPOSITE: *Crowland Abbey did not enjoy the peaceful existence intended for it.*

you stand and gaze upon these few beautiful remnants of the once proud building, you get a true sense of what it must have been like in those distant days of devout meditation, a devotion which has pervaded the history-laden walls with an aura of sanctity.

BARDNEY ABBEY
NR. LINCOLN, LINCOLNSHIRE
The Saint Who Came in From the Cold

King Aethelred of Mercia and his wife Queen Osthryd founded Bardney Abbey in AD 675 as a shrine to St Oswald (Osthryd's uncle), king of Northumberland, who had been killed in battle in AD 642. When the monastery was finished, St Oswald's body was divided between several religious foundations. His head went to the great abbey at Lindisfarne, his arms were sent to Bamburgh and the rest of him was brought to Bardney. In his *Ecclesiastical History of the English People* the venerable Bede (c.673–735) recalls that when the holy relics arrived at the gates of Bardney Abbey, the monks were dubious about Oswald's worthiness for sainthood. They refused to allow his remains into the abbey precincts, and so the cart carrying them was forced to stay outside the gates overnight. In the early hours of the morning, a great pillar of light shot skywards out of the coffin and the monks became convinced that Oswald was indeed a saint and welcomed his remains into the abbey. Tradition maintains that they removed the abbey's great doors so that such a mistake could never be made again.

Soon Bardney Abbey had become a place of pilgrimage, and for over 200 years visitors flocked to pay homage to St Oswald's bones. Then around the year 870, the Vikings arrived and saw the wealthy monasteries as ripe for plundering. Bardney Abbey was sacked, its monks slaughtered and its buildings destroyed. The shrine of St Oswald was desecrated and in 913 his bones were moved to Gloucester. The abbey lay forgotten until after the Norman Conquest, when Gilbert de Ghent, Lord of Bardney, founded a new monastery on the site in 1087. This lasted nearly 500 years before it was destroyed during the Dissolution of the Monasteries in 1538. All that now remains are traces of the walls and precincts.

JULIAN'S BOWER
ALKBOROUGH, LINCOLNSHIRE
The Mysterious Labyrinth

This mysterious maze sits on a small plateau and is cut into the turf of a hill just outside the village of Alkborough. It occupies a lovely spot and boasts commanding views across the convergence of the rivers Trent and Humber. Its exact age is uncertain, although the first mention of it is in 1697 when it was noticed by the Yorkshire antiquarian Abraham de la Pryme. Although there are claims that it is of Roman origin, the general consensus holds that it dates from the medieval period. It is a circular maze full of concentric paths, about 45cm (18in) wide, that turn back on themselves. Close up it is evidently a clever design that shows great intricacy in its creation.

It is not known for certain what the purpose of a maze was. Turf mazes often bore the name of 'Julian's Bower' or 'Walls of Troy', probably from the belief that Julius son of Aeneas – the legendary founder of Rome – brought maze games to Italy from Troy after its sacking by the Greeks.

Maze patterns were adopted by the early Church and may have been used for penitential purposes. Some cathedrals and larger churches have mazes on the marble floor tiles inside their main entrances. The centre of the maze was sometimes known as Jerusalem, and when pilgrims were unable to journey to the Holy Land, they would instead crawl the cathedral or church labyrinth on their knees. As a result, mazes came to be a Christian symbol that represented the path to salvation. Julian's Bower may have first been cut by monks from Walcott (a village about a mile distant from

BELOW: *The forlorn ruins of Grace Dieu Priory may well have been constructed from the broken up segments of an ancient stone circle.*

OPPOSITE: *Rushton Triangular Lodge stands as a striking testimony to the unshakable faith of the dedicated Catholic, Sir Thomas Tresham.*

the maze) and may have been intended for use in their penitential rituals. The monks would have crawled on hands and knees to gain forgiveness for whatever transgressions they had committed.

Following the Reformation in the 16th century it became a place of recreation, and records show that it was being used for May Eve celebrations as recently as the 1850s. The location and the views are truly lovely and it makes the perfect vantage point from which to watch the comings and goings on the river below, while at the same time enjoying the sun setting over the surrounding countryside.

GRACE DIEU PRIORY
LEICESTERSHIRE
Forlorn and Lonely Grace Dieu

Grace Dieu Priory, although little more than a forlorn ruin today, is a rare example of an Augustinian nunnery. It was founded in 1239/40 by Roesia de Verdun for 14 nuns and their prioress. It has been suggested that the nunnery was founded at this particular spot to break the hold that the old gods and pagan religions still had over those who lived in the neighbourhood. A solitary standing stone can still be seen on the opposite side of the brook across from the ruins, and at one time this would most certainly have been within the priory complex. There is evidence to suggest that the stone was one of 14 arranged in a circle and which, during the Dark Ages, may well have been significant to the beliefs of the local people. It is possible that the early Church strove to

either obliterate the previous beliefs or at least assimilate them into the Christian faith by breaking the stones up, and even incorporating them into the buildings of the nunnery.

It is not known for sure how many occupants would have lived at the priory at any one time during its 300-year history as a religious house, but it appears to have been a thriving community. The priory's days of glory ended in 1539 during the Dissolution of the Monasteries when the nuns were turned out and their prioress was given the paltry compensation of just 60 shillings for the loss of her estates.

One of the commissioners responsible for its dissolution was John Beaumont of Thringstone, who took advantage of his position to acquire Grace Dieu on extremely favourable terms, and he subsequently set about converting it into a suitable family home. It was here that his grandson, the dramatist Francis Beaumont, was born in 1584. The Beaumonts remained in possession until 1690 when they sold the house to a wealthy Leicestershire landowner, Sir Ambrose Phillips, whose short tenure saw the demolition of most of the remaining nunnery church in 1696. Over the century that followed, the property was abandoned and it fell into such disrepair that, by the time William Wordsworth visited in 1811, he was moved to comment on its decay and bemoaned what he called 'The ivied ruins of forlorn Grace Dieu.'

LEFT: *The Eleanor Cross at Geddington symbolises Edward I's love for his wife. He created a beautiful tomb for her in Westminster Abbey, as well as twelve stone crosses, one for each stop that the funeral procession made.*

Today, the Grace Dieu Trust is working hard to preserve the little that remains of the place, and hopes to eventually make it safe for public access. In the meantime it remains a wonderful spectacle. The ruins enjoy an eerie reputation locally, thanks to the activities of a phantom white lady who may be one of the nuns brought back perhaps by an ancient magic that still resonates from the shattered standing stones that were incorporated into the nunnery buildings.

ALL SAINTS' CHURCH
BRAUNSTON, LEICESTERSHIRE
The Celtic Mother Goddess

There is a curious relic outside All Saints' Church in Braunston, Leicestershire that may well predate the founding of the church. It is a crouching figure of an extremely ugly woman whose origins are uncertain. It appears that, until the early 1900s, she lay face down in the earth and was used as a step. It was only when renovation work was being carried out on the church that she was rediscovered and once more set upright against the wall of the church. A rather exposed position that has made her vulnerable to passing lawn mowers.

The figure is very curious indeed, possessing as she does a truly fierce aspect. She has bulging, large round eyes, a large tongue that thrusts from an equally immense mouth, and a series of rings around her neck, below which are just discernible sagging, hard-nippled breasts. It has been speculated that the figure was once part of earlier church masonry, but this is an unlikely premise because it is difficult to see how such a large, post-like stone could have fitted easily into the walls of the church. Another theory is that she was a boundary marker that once stood as a guardian over a pre-Roman tribal frontier. A local historian has wondered if she could possibly recall '…a pre-Christian place of worship amongst the forests of the marlstone country on the borders of Rutland and Leicestershire, where colonising Angles came late and settled sparsely?'

Expanding on this hypothesis, it has been suggested that she could be a depiction of a 2,000-year-old Celtic Earth Mother once worshipped in primitive fertility rites on the site of the church. Perhaps that is why she was toppled over to be left, face down and forgotten. The Celtic Mother Goddess was goddess of both sexuality and war and that may be why the features are both repulsive yet decidedly sexual in nature.

THE TRIANGULAR LODGE
RUSHTON, NORTHAMPTONSHIRE
A Statement of Faith

As you wander the lonely backwater roads that cut through the serenely beautiful Northamptonshire countryside, you stumble upon a curiously ostentatious building that has been described as 'the purest folly in the country'. It stands in the grounds of Rushton Hall, a late-15th century country manor house that was once the principal estate of the Tresham family.

An ardent Catholic, Sir Thomas Tresham conceived the idea for the Rushton Triangular Lodge while in prison for his religious beliefs. Upon his release in 1593, he set about designing a structure that would be both a clandestine declaration of his faith and a covert shrine to his suffering. The result was this remarkable three-sided, three-storied edifice constructed to commemorate architecturally the Holy Trinity and the Mass. Symbolic dates, emblems, shields, sculpted gargoyles and biblical quotations adorn the three exterior walls, each of which has three windows, topped by three gables over which looms a three-sided chimney, festooned with Tresham trefoils. On the entrance front is the inscription *Tres Testimonium Dant* ('There are Three that give witness'), which is a quote from the Gospel of St John that refers to the Holy Trinity. It is also a pun on Tresham's name, because his wife referred to him as 'Good Tres' in her letters.

THE ELEANOR CROSS
GEDDINGTON, NORTHAMPTONSHIRE
Symbol of Long Shanks's Grief

The devotion of Edward I to his Queen, Eleanor of Castile, is aptly demonstrated by the fact that he erected 12 crosses to her memory following her premature death in 1290. The couple's love for each other would border on legend and be remembered long after their deaths. According to a tradition written a hundred years afterwards, when Edward was on the 8th Crusade he was injured by an assassin's knife in Acre in 1272, Eleanor saved his life by sucking the poison from the infected wound. The two of them nearly always travelled together, so when she died unexpectedly at Harby in Nottinghamshire, the King was beside himself with grief. Indeed, some chroniclers maintain that Edward's rule became a lot harsher following the death of his beloved wife.

Her body was first taken to St Catherine's Priory at nearby Lincoln and her entrails were interred at Lincoln Cathedral. Her embalmed body was then taken in procession to London, a journey that took 12 days. Edward ordered that a large stone cross was to be erected at every place that they made an overnight stop. Only three of these Eleanor Crosses now survive. The Puritan sentiments of Cromwell's soldiers in the 1660s were responsible for the destruction of all the others. The one at Geddington, which is widely considered to be the best in both architecture and state of preservation, dates from 1294, and stands as lasting testament to the love of Edward I for his wife.

The Devil's Playground, Sleeping Stones and the Plague Village

Here rests his head upon the lap of Earth
A Youth to Fortune and to Fame unknown.
Fair Science frown'd not on his humble birth,
And Melancholy mark'd him for her own.
Large was his bounty, and his soul sincere,
Heav'n did a recompense as largely send:
He gave to Mis'ry all he had, a tear,
He gain'd from Heav'n ('twas all he wish'd) a friend.

From 'Elegy written in a country churchyard'
by Thomas Gray (1716-1771)

SHROPSHIRE, STAFFORDSHIRE & DERBYSHIRE

The counties of Staffordshire, Cheshire, Derbyshire and Shropshire offer an intriguing contrast of beautiful scenery and industrial landscapes. The coal, iron and other mineral deposits that were mined here helped fuel the Industrial Revolution and the expansion of the British Empire, and have left visible scars across the region. Many of the chimneys and kilns that once pumped pollutants into the atmosphere are today silent. Yet, they possess an aura of mystery and detachment that is vaguely reminiscent of that found at some of Britain's more ancient monuments. Within this industrial heartland, however, one also finds the awesome beauty of the Peak District, where rocky crags rise from rugged moorlands, and underground caverns conceal magical displays of stalactites and stalagmites. Elsewhere, gentle valleys, through which babble tranquil streams and rivers, are home to

PAGE 96: *The Romans were the first to recognise that St Anne's Well had sacred properties.*

PREVIOUS PAGE: *The massive boulders that make up the Stiperstones have many legends attached to them, nearly all of which see the Devil's hand in their construction.*

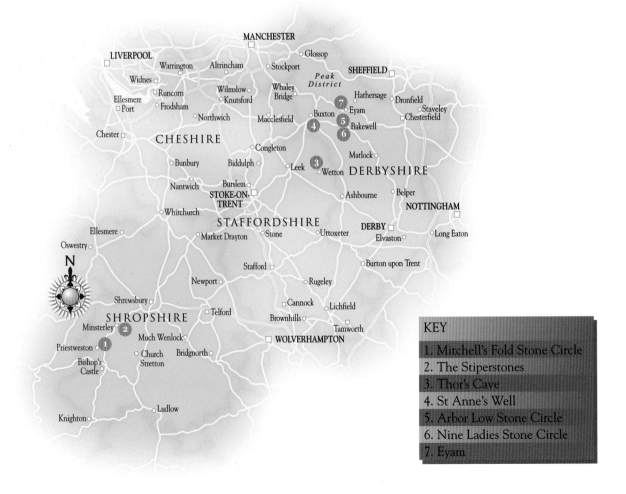

KEY
1. Mitchell's Fold Stone Circle
2. The Stiperstones
3. Thor's Cave
4. St Anne's Well
5. Arbor Low Stone Circle
6. Nine Ladies Stone Circle
7. Eyam

sacred sites whose origins are long forgotten. All in all, it is a landscape where the myths and legends of the distant past sit side by side with the folklore of more recent events.

MITCHELL'S FOLD STONE CIRCLE
Nr. Priestweston, Shropshire
A Bronze Age Place of Worship

Mitchell's Fold Stone Circle (also known as Medjices Fold and Madges Pinfold) sits proudly in a high saddle on the long ridge of Stapeley Hill, 305m (1,000ft) above sea level and provides stunning views across the Welsh border. It dates from approximately 2000 to 1400 BC and was erected by local Bronze Age communities probably for a ritual or ceremonial purpose. Although only 14 of its original 30 stones now survive, its exposed position is truly awesome, and it is still possible to feel that you really are in the middle of something special and mystical.

Local legend tells that a giant used to live at the circle and that he possessed a cow that yielded an unceasing supply of milk. One day a wicked witch asked the cow for some milk, and the cow, who evidently was not up on the wiles of

ABOVE: *Only 14 of the original 30 stones now survive at Mitchell's Fold Stone Circle, but their exposed location helps make them both mystical and awe-inspiring.*

witches, readily agreed. The witch milked the cow into a sieve and eventually even its ceaseless supply ran out. The cow disappeared from the district never to be seen again. The witch was turned to stone for her crime and may well be the impressive 1.8m (6ft) high monolith. The local people set a circle of other stones around her to prevent her from ever escaping. Another tradition maintains that King Arthur even came to this windswept place and it was from one of the stones that he drew Excalibur.

THE STIPERSTONES
Nr. Minsterley, Shropshire
Where the Devil Holds Court

These massive boulders are scattered along the spine of a rocky ridge near to the English and Welsh border and several legends exist to explain how they came to be there. The common theme that runs through each is that the Devil was

ABOVE: *Legend claims that the Stiperstones came into existence when the Devil dropped his heavy load on a hot and sunny day.*

THOR'S CAVE
NR. WHETTON, STAFFORDSHIRE
An Eye onto a Distant World

Thor's Cave is the most awe-inspiring and impressive sight of the Manifold Valley. The huge limestone bluff in which it is set looms over the landscape high above the river, and the mouth of the cave, which gapes open an amazing 9m (30ft) high and 7m (23ft) wide, is clearly visible from several miles around. Since it is 76m (250ft) up, thankfully steps have been built to enable a reasonably easy ascent and once inside you are pitched into a twilight world that is both eerie and mystical. Excavations have shown that the cave was occupied as long as 10,000 years ago and this occupation probably continued until Roman or Saxon times, making it one of the oldest sites of human activity in the Peak District. One of the great mysteries concerning the cave is why it should be named after the Norse God, Thor, and no satisfactory explanation has ever been given. It may be that the name commemorates a long-held local tradition that some form of monster or demon dwelt within the cave. The fact that it is also known in the area as 'Fiend's Hole', would seem to give some credence to this theory. But theories as to the origins of the name aside, this is a truly remarkable place, a mystical world of shadow, where the spirits of its long-ago residents still seem to linger and where you can gaze out across the beautiful Manifold Valley.

ST ANNE'S WELL
BUXTON, DERBYSHIRE
A Sacred Spring

St Anne's Well was for centuries a place of pilgrimage, a holy spot to which the faithful would flock in search of cures for all manner of ailments. However, long before the medieval pilgrims made their weary way to take the waters and immerse themselves in the awe-inspiring aura of the place, the Romans had come to the region in search of lead and silver. They discovered a revered spring and named the settlement which they established around it Aquae Arnemetiae. Arnemetia was a Celtic name which translates as 'in front of a grove'. Thus the Roman name literally meant 'water of she who dwells against the sacred grove'.

Centuries later when the early Celtic Christian missionaries followed in the Romans' footsteps, they were only too happy, even eager, to absorb the ancient and more

somehow involved in their formation. The largest of the crags is known as the Devil's Chair. Local tradition has it that long ago the Devil was carrying rocks in his apron with which he intended to fill a valley called 'Hell's Gutter'. However, he became wearied by the hot sun, and sat down to rest. When he stood up again the strings of his apron snapped and the rocks tumbled onto the ground. Satan cursed and left the boulders where they had fallen and headed back to hell. It is claimed that when a mist swirls around the Devil's Chair, Satan and a coven of witches are meeting and bad deeds are afoot. Another version of the story says that the Devil was flying over the area one day when he spied a giantess trying to carry off his chair in her apron. Furious he swooped down and cut clean through her apron strings, causing the boulders to crash to earth where they now lie. Ever since, the devil is said to return regularly to sit on the rocks and scrutinize the area around for any evil that he can do. A final version tells of an ancient prophecy which stated that should the stones sink into the ground then England would fall into ruin. Desperate to see this happen sooner rather than later the Devil sat in his chair and attempted to push it into the earth. Fortunately, the ground proved too hard and England was spared!

established beliefs into their own faith, and so the goddess Arnemetia became Christianized as St Anne. St Anne was, according to legend, the mother of Mary and thus the Matriarch of the Holy Family. Her cult flourished in England between the early 14th and mid-16th centuries. She became particularly popular with illiterate peasants, amongst whom she was seen as the powerful grandmother figure who was able to intercede on their behalf with her grandson, Jesus. To the bourgeoisie she came to personify family values and was seen as a holy mother and grandmother, contentedly presiding over a family of well-brought-up daughters and grandsons. She was frequently depicted holding a book, with which she was teaching the young Virgin Mary to read, and so she became identified with education, especially for women.

By 1540, at least 40 churches and chapels in England were under her patronage, the majority being dedicated or re-dedicated over the previous two centuries, and major shrines had been established in her honour at Wood-Plumpton in Lancashire and, most importantly, at Buxton. However, the dedication of Buxton's pagan healing spring to her was of far earlier date, and is thought to be one of the earliest, if not the earliest, in England. There is a medieval legend which tells of an ancient statue being found in the well. Although this may have been a statue of the Celtic goddess Arnemetia, the monks may have either mistook it for St Anne or, more probably, deliberately claimed it was St Anne to prove the ancient pedigree of their shrine. This medieval shrine stood to the east of the spring site and may well have had an antechapel that bestrode the spring. There may have been a stone bath in which the pilgrims could immerse themselves, and by which votive offerings could have been left showing depictions of the afflicted body parts which it was hoped St Anne would help to cure. If a cure was obtained, then crutches or other symbols of the disease or affliction would be left at the shrine to demonstrate the potency of the healing waters.

Following the Reformation in the 16th century, the shrine was secularized and passed into the hands of the Cavendish family, later to become the Dukes of Devonshire. However, pilgrims continued to visit, including the ill-fated Mary, Queen of Scots, who came here while being held a prisoner

BELOW: *Thor's Cave is a prominent landmark of the Manifold Valley and may have been occupied as long as 10,000 years ago.*

A WELL OF
LIVING WATERS

at nearby Chatsworth, hoping that the waters would cure her chronic rheumatism.

In the 18th century the Dukes of Devonshire became extremely rich, largely as a result of copper and lead mining, and the 5th duke, anxious to compete with the popularity of Bath, embarked upon an ambitious building programme that effectively ended any sense of sacred mysticism at St Anne's Well.

Today, Buxton Spa Water is sold throughout the world, although it is freely available from the modern St Anne's Well that stands opposite the grandiose Crescent. Although not sited where the sacred spring once flowed, and resembling a glorified drinking fountain, it still serves as a reminder of the ancient sanctity of these waters at a Celtic site that the Romans were suitably impressed with, and which the Christian Church chose to adopt as a shrine to the woman who, legends holds, sat as the saintly matriarch at the head of the Holy Family.

ARBOR LOW STONE CIRCLE
Nr. Bakewell, Derbyshire
The Stonehenge of the North

Arbor Low (a corruption of Eorthburgh Hlaw, meaning 'Earthwork Mound') is considered the finest Stone Age 'henge' monument in the North of England and is often referred to as the Stonehenge of the North. It is the only circle in Derbyshire to be built from limestone and it occupies a high point some 375m (1,230ft) above sea level. It dates back to the Neolithic/early Bronze Age and is believed to have been built around 2500 BC. One of the surprises of this mysterious henge is that all the stones lie flat. It is not known whether the stones ever stood upright, although there is a theory that the early Christians were

responsible for toppling them in order to demonstrate the superiority of their religion over an older faith.

Although no one knows for certain why Arbor Low was constructed, there is a tradition that is was intended as a sacred burial place for priests, chieftains and other important people. It has also been suggested that the site was used as a place of human sacrifice, although proof for either theory is inconclusive.

What is certain is that Arbor Low has something of a sinister reputation, and it is claimed that few local people will venture near the stones when darkness has fallen. In his *Romances of the Peak*, W. M. Turner told how he paid a visit to the site in 1897. As he left he was accosted by a young herdsman who told him of a local tradition that 'there had been a battle there and people had been buried about the place'. He also told him that 'the folks round about never go that way at night for fear of boggarts'. A 'boggart' was an evil, mischievous spirit that, in the case of Arbor Low, was fearsome looking and possessed very sharp, long, bright yellow teeth. Its most sinister habit was that of following people home and crawling into their beds.

Wicked spirits aside, Arbor Low is a splendid and airy site and to stand on its soaring heights and feel the wind on your face is to immerse yourself in the true spirit of the place. The claim that 50 ley lines are believed to pass through the site adds a genuinely spellbinding quality to this ancient and mysterious place.

OPPOSITE: *Worshippers once flocked in their thousands to partake of the curative waters of Buxton's St Anne's Well.*

BELOW: *The slumbering stones of Arbor Low belie a local reputation that is truly sinister.*

NINE LADIES STONE CIRCLE
Nr. Bakewell, Derbyshire
Where Morris Men See In May Day

The gritstone expanse of Stanton Moor has been described as being 'like a lost world' and was evidently a sacred landscape in the Stone and Bronze Ages. Scattered amongst the heather and birch are the remnants of over 70 Bronze Age barrows and over five stone circles, of which the most famous is undoubtedly the Nine Ladies. It consists of a complete ring of nine evenly spaced, heavily weathered stones, 10.5m (35ft) in diameter. It is a mysterious and evocative site that casts a powerful spell, especially as dusk descends over the surrounding woodland and the sun sinks below the horizon, casting long shadows that seem to stretch back into the foggy mists of time. Indeed, the plateau on which the circle stands is known to have been in use between 2000 and 1500 BC and was probably a site of considerable religious significance. Today, the grass at the centre of the ring is blackened by the numerous fires lit by those who come to absorb the spiritual energy of this tranquil spot, and who in so doing have unthinkingly endangered the stones since the heat from the fires can cause their surfaces to crack, while the effect of their footsteps is to erode the surrounding soil.

Some 40m (135ft) to the south-west of the circle stands a lone monolith around which has gathered a colourful tale to account for the origin of the stone circle. Known as the 'King Stone' this is reputedly a petrified fiddler whose bow led nine maidens to enjoy a merry jig on the exposed summit one long-ago Sabbath and, as punishment, he and the dancers were turned to stone. It is a traditional tale often used to explain the origins of pagan stone circles, but the appeal of this particular circle seems to grow with each passing year and the site is a frequent meeting place for modern pagans as well as witches. At dawn on May Day the Derby Morris Men make the trek to the moor and dance among the stones for the delectation of those early risers who follow them to this place of ancient mystery.

EYAM
Derbyshire
The Plague Village

The village of Eyam nestles in a sleepy hollow from which brooding hills climb steeply onto high moorland. It is a remote and isolated village where poignant reminders of a long ago tragedy are scattered about the gardens, displayed upon the walls of the pretty stone cottages or else lie peacefully in nearby fields.

Next to the village church stands a line of houses known as 'Plague Cottages'. Here in 1665 there lodged at the home

BELOW: *The scattered stones of the Nine Ladies Stone Circle stand upon the gritstone expanse of Stanton Moor and were once a site of religious significance.*

of Mary Cooper a tailor named George Viccars. In the September of that year he received from London a parcel of damp cloth, which he spread out to dry before the fire. Unbeknown to him he released into the village, plague-carrying fleas whose bite would, over the next 12 months, decimate the small community. Viccars himself was the first victim and he was closely followed by his landlady's son, Edward Cooper.

By October the pestilence was raging and, under the leadership of their vicar, William Mompesson, the residents of Eyam made the brave decision to cut themselves off from the outside world in order to prevent the contagion from spreading throughout the district. Supplies were left at a well on the outskirts of the village that is today known as 'Mompesson's Well', the stones of which still bear the hollows where payment was placed in pools of vinegar in order to cleanse the tainted currency.

As the Plague took hold and decimated the villagers it was decided to hold the church services outdoors at nearby Cucklett Delf to minimize the spread of the disease. The church itself was closed, and families buried their dead in their own gardens or in surrounding fields. At nearby Riley – a plot of land on the top of a hill adjoining the eastern edge

BELOW: *Eyam Hall, along with all the houses in Eyam, was cut off from the surrounding area in a selfless act by the villagers to prevent the plague from decimating other communities.*

of Eyam – Elizabeth Hancock buried her husband and six children in the space of eight days. The Riley Graves, as they are known, can still be seen today and are a poignant reminder of the terrible grief this poor woman must have experienced. By the time the final victim died on 1st November 1666, the outbreak had claimed the lives of 260 people, possibly a third of the village's population. One of the last fatalities was Catherine Mompesson, the vicar's wife, who died on 25th August. She had loyally stayed with her husband in order to tend the sick.

Eyam has not forgotten those former residents who strove to prevent the Plague from spreading outside their village. Memorial plaques on the cottage walls that list the names of those who died and weathered tombstones strewn about the village testify to the devastation wreaked on the tiny community. Yet the village is a very spiritual and uplifting place, where the Christian convictions and heroic sacrifice made by those people is truly inspiring. Their actions are remembered each year on Plague Sunday (the last Sunday in August) with a memorial service in Cucklett Delf, and by decorating Catherine Mompesson's grave in Eyam churchyard with a rose entwined wreath. The church itself dates back to the 13th century and has many points of interest, such as a Plague victim's book, Mompesson's chair, wall paintings and Jacobean wood carvings, while the Peak District's best-preserved Saxon Cross, dating back to the 7th century, graces the churchyard.

Mysterious Landscapes Where Legends Abound

Who are these coming to sacrifice?
To what green altar, O mysterious priest,
Lead'st thou that heifer lowing at the skies,
And all her silken flanks with garlands drest?
What little town by river or sea-shore,
Or mountain-built with peaceful citadel,
Is emptied of its folk, this pious morn?
And, little town, thy streets for evermore
Will silent be; and not a soul, to tell
Why thou art desolate, can e'er return.

FROM 'ODE ON A GRECIAN URN'
BY JOHN KEATS (1795–1821)

WALES

Even centuries of political oppression have not managed to crush the Welsh imagination. Its roots are buried so deeply in the Celtic past that no invader could ever destroy it. Even today the remote, brooding mountains, weatherbeaten coastlines, dark, sinister lakes and languorous beaches, still have the power to stir the spirit and free the mind. The people of Wales are in fact the ancient Britons who were driven westwards by the Saxon invaders who, unable and unwilling to understand the

PAGE 106: *St Govan's Chapel, where tradition has it that no mortal can count the steps that lead to it.*

PREVIOUS PAGE: *Fairies looking like 'little children … with red caps' are sometimes seen weaving around the mysterious stones of Pentre Ifan.*

KEY
1. Bardsey Island
2. St Winifred's Well
3. Valle Crucis Abbey
4. Pentre Ifan, Nr Nevan
5. St David's Cathedral
6. The Carew Cross
7. St Govan's Chapel
8. Kenfig Pool
9. Skirrid Mountain

language of those whose lands they had taken, called them Welsh which was their word for 'foreigner'. As this defeated people settled into their mountain fastness, they dreamt of the day when they would return to reclaim what was rightfully theirs. They called themselves Cymry, meaning 'comrades', and the rugged wilds of their mountainous domain they named Cymru, meaning 'for their land'. Theirs is a land where legends abound, a land of mystery where the oral tradition has ensured that the deeds of the past are never forgotten. For, as far as all true Welshmen are concerned, Wales was, is and always will be *hen wlad fy nhadau*, 'the land of my fathers'.

BARDSEY ISLAND
LYN PENINSULA, NORTH WALES
The Island of the Saints
Situated off the tip of the Llyn Peninsula, Bardsey Island has long being considered a holy and sacred place. It is known locally as Ynys Enlli, 'the Island of the Currents', on account of the unpredictable tides between it and the mainland. In AD 516 the Breton saint, Cadfan established what was probably the first monastic community in Wales on the island. Soon, despite the treacherous crossing, it became a popular place of pilgrimage and three visits to it were considered the equal of one to Rome.

Eventually, the belief sprang up that if someone was buried on Bardsey they would be spared the torments of hell, no matter how wicked they had been in life! It therefore

BELOW: *So holy was Bardsey Island once thought to be that it was once claimed that 20,000 saints lay buried beneath its turfs.*

became the cherished desire of devout Christians in North Wales to be laid to rest there, and by the late Middle Ages it was said that 20,000 saints lay buried on this holiest of islands. An Augustinian abbey dedicated to St Mary was established to cater for both the temporal and spiritual needs of the pilgrims who flocked to Bardsey.

The cells and chapels have long since vanished and only a handful of ruins, mingled with the bones of Celtic saints, remain to remind us of the island's sacred past. Yet Bardsey is still a place of refuge. In 2004 it celebrated 18 years as a National Nature Reserve, providing a peaceful sanctuary for marine animals, plants and an amazing variety of birds. It is also reputed to be the final resting place of Merlin, who is said to sleep in a cave awaiting the day when Britain is in peril when he will awake and come to her rescue.

It is this blend of legend, landscape and history that makes a trip to Bardsey Island so rewarding. It is not difficult to imagine those medieval pilgrims crammed into small wooden boats being rowed across from the mainland, nervously aware of the potentially fatal power of the tides around them. You can almost sense their euphoria as, with the dangerous crossing over, they stepped eagerly onto the shoreline of the place they knew simply as 'the island of saints'.

ST WINIFRED'S WELL
HOLYWELL, FLINTSHIRE
Holy Heads and a Healing Well
Gazing into the ominous waters of a deep well or watching the foaming torrents of a raging river, you can begin to understand why our ancestors came to see water as such an awe-inspiring and fearsome commodity – essential to life, yet

it was also able to kill and destroy. The ancient peoples came to see springs, wells and rivers as either portals to the otherworld, or as dwelling places for the gods themselves. As such they became centres of worship, about which legends were told and at which offerings and sacrifices were made. When the Christian missionaries began spreading their message across Europe, rather than desecrate these shrines they chose instead to merge them into their own religion. Of course they ensured that whatever pagan wonders were said to have occurred around them were eclipsed by the miraculous actions of their own saints. Whereas it was customary for the Celts to hack the heads from vanquished enemies and fling them into rivers or wells as offerings to their water deities, the Christian missionaries used the powerful symbolism of the restoration of a decapitated head to illustrate how their saints were able to overcome the powers of the pagan gods. Just such a tale lies behind the foundation of St Winifred's shrine.

The well that is situated within the shrine is widely regarded as the finest surviving example of a medieval holy well in Britain, with an unbroken tradition of pilgrimage that stretches back almost a thousand years. Its origins are said to date from the 7th century, when Winifrid, or Gwenffrwd to use her actual name, a well-connected and noble young lady, was visited one day by a local chieftain named Caradoc. Smitten by her beauty, the lustful chieftain attempted to seduce the saintly Gwenffrwd, but when she rejected his advances he flew into a violent rage and attempted to force himself upon her. Girding up her skirts, Gwenffrwd dodged past her would-be attacker and headed off in the direction of a nearby chapel, where her uncle St Beuno was preaching. As she ran down the hill towards it, Caradoc caught up with her, drew his sword and swung it with such ferocity that he cleaved Gwenffrwd's head clean

ABOVE: *Valle Crucis Abbey was once one of the wealthiest foundations in Wales. Today its ruins nestle in peaceful seclusion beneath the shadow of the Berwyn Mountains.*

OPPOSITE: *Kings and commoners alike have flocked to bathe in the waters of St Winifered's Holy Well.*

off her body. But justice came swiftly, for there came a great roar from beneath the ground and the next moment the earth opened and swallowed Caradoc. Gwenffrwd's head, meanwhile, continued rolling down the hill and where it finally came to rest a spring gushed forth from the earth. Alerted by the commotion, St Beuno came to his niece's aid, and picking up the head replaced it on her shoulders and restored her to life.

By 1155 the shrine, set into the hillside from where the miraculous water was said to have sprung forth, had become an important place of pilgrimage. Richard I is believed to have come here to pray for his Crusade, as did Henry V before and after his victory at Agincourt. Henry Tudor prayed at the shrine before setting off to meet Richard III at the battle of Bosworth, and returned as Henry VII to give thanks for his victory. James II, desperate for a male heir, brought his Queen, Mary of Modena, here in 1686. His prayers were answered two years later, though not quite as he had anticipated, for the birth of their son (who was eventually known as the 'Old Pretender') also lost James his crown, since there could be no Catholic heir to the throne. That great man of letters Dr Samuel Johnson also visited and found himself moved to prudish indignation by the lewd indecency of a woman he witnessed bathing in the healing waters.

Even today pilgrims continue to make the journey to this tranquil and sacred spot, which sits uneasily with the industrial units that make up its nearest neighbours. Sadly, however, the spring that for centuries gushed forth at an unfaltering 3,000 gallons per minute was interrupted by local mining operations in 1917. The unfortunate situation was resolved, although the bubbling spring that visitors see today is actually fed by a concealed pipe connected to Holywell's municipal water supply.

Whatever the source of its water, there is no doubt that St Winifred's Well remains a special and tranquil place to

House, with its beautifully delicate rib-vaulted roof, and the exquisite West Front, with its elaborately carved doorway, beautiful rose window and 14th-century inscription, 'Abbot Adams carried out this work; may he rest in peace. Amen.'

The wealth of the abbey increased greatly throughout the 15th century, which was a period that saw a gradual relaxing of the Cistercians' adherence to austerity. Indeed, by the end of the century poets were openly praising the hospitality of its abbots. But hospitality was no guard against the wishes of Henry VIII and in 1537 the abbey was dissolved. Thereafter its buildings rapidly fell into disrepair.

Many of the ruins were roofed again towards the end of the 18th century, and were pressed into use as a farm. In the 19th century interest was belatedly shown once more in what is a delightful piece of rural paradise. Around this time the Rev. Owen, custodian of the abbey, began excavation and clearance work on the site in the course of which he stumbled upon some interesting finds. One of the more fascinating of these discoveries was a 13th-century copy of the Koran, which may well have been brought back from the Crusades by one of the knights whose tombs can be seen at the abbey.

Other finds were of Roman and Saxon origin and suggested that a previous building may well have stood on the site, which in turn has in recent years led to some intriguing speculation that links the abbey's site to that most legendary of Dark Age figures, King Arthur. It has been suggested that the site may well have been the place where St Collen, after whom Llangollen is named, founded a chapel, which may well have been the location of the real Glastonbury (see page 21), around which so much Arthurian lore and legend hangs.

Interestingly, at the side of the A542 out of Llangollen, and near to Valle Crucis Abbey, is Eliseg's Pillar, the most important Dark Age artefact in the British Isles. It was erected by Concenn, ruler of Powys in the 9th century, and commemorates his great grandfather Eliseg, who prevented Powys from falling into the hands of the Saxons. The inscriptions that were placed on it have long since been worn away and are no longer visible. But fortunately the antiquarian Elfyn Llwyd, who toured the area in the late 17th century, faithfully copied the inscriptions down. It is intriguing that many of them are today associated with the

which pilgrim's still journey, just as they have done for nigh on a thousand years. In the outer pool they still kneel upon the stone of St Beuno on which he is said to have taught Gwenffrwd and from which he reputedly said goodbye to her. A number of stones in the valley below are said to be stained with her blood, and a red-tinged fragrant moss that grows at the bottom of the well is known as St Winifrid's hair.

VALLE CRUCIS ABBEY
Nr. Llangollen, Denbighshire
A Sacred Spot in Rural Tranquillity

Valle Crucis, the 'Valley of the Cross', lies in the shadow of the Berwyn Mountains and nestles amidst picturesque lush, green fields. In medieval times this was a secluded spot and its remoteness made it an ideal place for the austere Cistercian monks, who purposely sought wild and lonely places in which to devote themselves to God. Their abbey was established in 1201 and added to a century later. It has fared well against the ravages of time, and many of its original features are still visible. These include the Chapter

LEFT: *Pentre Ifan is one of many sites in Wales where the spirits of those who passed through here long ago can still be sensed.*

OPPOSITE: *St David's Cathedral occupies a peaceful setting in a woody dell and commemorates the patron saint of Wales.*

Arthurian legends. A fact that might just lend credence to Valle Crucis's claim of links to the mythical king.

PENTRE IFAN
Nr. Nevern, Pembrokeshire
Laid to Rest in a Bygone Age

Dating from at least 3500 BC, Pentre Ifan is dramatically placed on the slopes of a grassy ridge and consists of a huge capstone that weighs over 16 tons, which is delicately poised on top of three uprights that lift its sombre bulk 2.5m (8ft) off the ground. It is probably all that remains of a chambered tomb for the communal burial of the dead that would have been used for a time before being sealed. Excavations at the site have revealed that the burial chamber originally lay within a shallow oval pit, and that it was covered by a mound of earth that extended for some 36.5m (120ft).

The overall air of mystery that pervades the site is greatly enhanced by a local tradition that fairies, looking like 'little children in clothes like soldiers' clothes and with red caps', are sometimes seen at the site. There is also a theory that suggests that Pentre Ifan was once a favoured place of the Druids who had a flourishing school for neophytes in the oak groves around the site. Pentre Ifan, far from being a place of interment, formed a darkened chamber in which novices were placed for a certain number of days as part of their initiation into the mysterious order.

It is possible to speculate for hours on end as to the purpose and origins of enigmatic and ancient places such as this. They stand as proud monuments to a forgotten people who passed this way long ago and whose spirits live on in the mysterious sites that they have left behind them.

ST DAVID'S CATHEDRAL,
St David's, Pembrokeshire
Patron Saint of Wales and His Holy Mother

During the 6th century, monasteries began to flourish all

over the Celtic fringe of western Europe. St David was born in this century near, it is thought, to where the cathedral now stands. In adulthood he embraced the lifestyle of an abstemious Celtic monk and encouraged his followers to do likewise. In the 6th century he founded the monastery of Menevia on the site now occupied by the present cathedral. David was actually killed by Viking raiders towards the end of the century, and some came to see his death as divine retribution for eating meat. The frugal lifestyle of the Celtic priesthood adhered to a strictly vegetarian diet and David was the first bishop to disregard this rule. Menevia was sacked several times by Viking raiders and all traces of it have now vanished. David was canonized by Pope Calixtus (1119–1124), whose declaration that two pilgrimages to Menevia were equal to one pilgrimage to Rome, ensured that this lovely spot, situated in a tranquil wooded valley, became a popular destination for pilgrims. They came seeking St David's intervention to ensure them speedy entrance to heaven. Others arrived to ask for the saint's intervention in assisting them to achieve more earthly rewards. Henry II, for example, stopped off in September 1171 to pray for victory in Ireland and returned again on Easter Monday 1172 to give thanks for it.

The present cathedral dates from around 1180, but the amount of pilgrim traffic that David's canonization brought and the wealth that it generated meant that by 1275 Bishop Richard de Carew was able to construct a new shrine for the saint's relics. In turn this further swelled the cathedral coffers which made possible a lavish programme of rebuilding and expansion. The shrine itself remains in the cathedral to this day and is located in the lovely Trinity Chapel. The cathedral has a very ancient feel to it and its carved wooden suspended ceiling is regarded as the finest of its kind in existence, while the painted wooden ceiling and vaulting beneath the tower is absolutely breathtaking.

On the windswept coast near to the cathedral is St Non's Well, standing on the site where St David was reputedly born. St Non or St Nona was the mother of St David.

LEFT: *The exquisite 11th century Carew Cross in Pembrokeshire may well be a monument to a former ruler of this region of Wales.*

According to legend, when she was in the last stages of her pregnancy she found herself out alone one night on the coast during a ferocious storm. She went into labour and where the child, David, was born a spring emerged, which later became St Non's Well. As a result of its miraculous origins this well has long held the reputation of being a healing well. About a hundred yards away from it are the ruins of St Non's chapel, occupying a truly idyllic setting which is actually within a stone circle. Thus it can be seen how the Christian religion, seeking to absorb an earlier Celtic tradition, chose to merge this ancient and mysterious site with the legend of St David and bestowed upon it a feeling of genuine sanctity that still holds sway over this picturesque and awe-inspiring part of Britain.

THE CAREW CROSS
Nr. Pembroke, Pembrokeshire
A Fine Early Christian Monument
Guarding the entrance to the hauntingly beautiful ruins of Carew Castle, the 11th-century Carew Cross is one of the three finest early Christian monuments in Wales (the others being at Nevern and Maen Achwyfan). The cross is 4m (13ft) high and was constructed in two separate sections. The upper segment has a Celtic wheel-shaped cross and short neck, and fits into a lower shaft, the face of which is inlaid with fine Celtic knotwork and interlaced ribbon pattern, its two sides displaying different variations that also reflect Scandinavian influences. The cross's origins go back to pre-Norman Wales when the country was ruled by powerful, independent princes. The cross can be dated from a crude Latin inscription halfway down one side, which translates as 'King Maredudd, son of Edwin'. Maredudd and his brother became joint rulers of the kingdom of Duheubarth in south-west Wales in 1033. However, Maredudd was killed in battle two years later and the Carew Cross is believed to be his royal monument.

ST GOVAN'S CHAPEL
NR. BUSHERTON, PEMBROKESHIRE
Sea-swept Sanctity

Despite the unholy proximity of a military firing range, St Govan's chapel is a truly spiritual place where legend and nature combine to create a sea-sprayed haven of magic and mystery set amidst some of the wildest and most rugged scenery imaginable. Dwarfed by the cliffs of the Pembrokeshire coast, it nestles securely in a rocky cleft, washed by wild waves and battered by savage winter gales that howl across the grey sea and hurl themselves with demonic fury at its ancient walls. You reach the little chapel by a flight of timeworn, uneven stone steps that tumble steeply between the crumbling rock-face, then squeeze through the solid bulk of several huge boulders to find yourself in a Spartan interior where a soothing aura of peaceful detachment washes over you.

Historically, St Govan (whose real name was Gobham or Gobban) is said to have lived in the 6th century and is thought to have been the abbot of a monastery at Dairinis in Wexford, on Ireland's west coast. One day, he was sailing along the Pembrokeshire coast, possibly on his way to visit a Welsh abbot, when his vessel was attacked by pirates intent on capturing him, no doubt realizing that such a high-placed cleric would fetch a hefty ransom. With the scurvy brigands in hot pursuit, Gobham headed for the coast. Suddenly a fissure opened in the rock before him and then closed behind him until the danger had passed. Gobham, however, was so overcome by guilt at his cowardice that he vowed to spend the rest of his days as a hermit and duly built a cell at the spot where divine

intervention had thwarted the pirates' ambitions. True to his word, the holy hermit saw out his days at this rugged location and, when he died, was buried beneath the stone altar around which his followers built the picturesque little chapel, parts of which may well date back to the 6th century, although most of it was built in the 11th century.

The moment you begin the precarious descent to the chapel you walk upon the legends that surround it, for tradition asserts that no mortal can ever count the number of steps accurately. Certainly, the tally on the ascent rarely agrees with that of the descent, although cynics might argue that the reason for this discrepancy lies with the irregularity of the steps. Behind the chapel's ancient stone altar there is a tiny cell, the rock of which bears a series of rib-like features said to be the imprint left by Gobham's body as he lay hidden from the pirates. It is also claimed that those who make a wish as they enter this fissure will have it granted if they are able to turn around inside it.

Amongst the immense boulders that litter the cove as it plunges from the chapel towards the pounding white foam of the sea beneath, there stands a large stone known as 'The Bell Rock'. It is said that Gobham was given a silver bell that was stolen from its tower by pirates. The saint prayed for its return, whereupon the angels retrieved it and secured it safely inside this large boulder. Whenever Gobham tapped the rock it would give out a clear note, which sounded a thousand times louder than the original bell. One

BELOW: *The sea-sprayed location of the tiny St Govan's chapel lends it an aura of detachment. To cross its threshold is to step back in time.*

ABOVE: *Skirrid Mountain is Wales's holy mountain that local tradition maintains was split in two by a bolt of lightning at the exact moment Christ died upon the cross.*

final legend of dubious authenticity suggests that St Govan may well have been Sir Gawain, the nephew of King Arthur. It is said that following his uncle's death he retired to live out his days at this isolated spot. However, since several Arthurian tales place Gawain's death before Arthur's last battle the tradition can be safely dismissed as wishful speculation fed by little more than the two names sharing a common first letter.

KENFIG POOL
NR. PORTHCAWL, GLAMORGAN
A Lost City Beneath the Waters

Legends and mysteries aplenty wash around this lovely pool, which now sits at the heart of the Kenfig Nature Reserve. Local tradition maintains that it is fed by seven springs, that it is bottomless, and that it contains a whirlpool that will drag the unwary down to a watery death. In reality its deepest section is around 4m (13ft) in depth, and the thick weeds that carpet its bed are probably responsible for pulling under those who have lost their lives here. There is an old tradition that the remains of a lost city

descendants in the seventh generation.

The couple lived to see their family grow in number until eventually they formed the entire population of the city. But then the first child of the seventh generation was born, and that night the disembodied voice was once again heard echoing through the city streets warning that vengeance had come. Sure enough there came a mighty roar, and moments later the whole town had vanished to be replaced by the tranquil waters of Kenfig Pool. No one escaped the disaster and thereafter the pool became a haunted spot. There is a long-held tradition that if you stand on its shores, in a quiet moment you might hear the mournful knell of the town's church bells. It is also said that three 'Devil's Chimney's' can sometimes be seen jutting out from the surface belching sulphurous fumes into the atmosphere.

SKIRRID MOUNTAIN
NR. LLANFIHANGEL CRUCORNEY, GWENT
The Mysterious Holy Mountain of Wales

The Skirrid Mountain, also known as St Michael's Mount and the Holy Mountain, is a prominent local landmark that is visible for miles around. Its majestic summit looms skyward and peaks at 486m (1,595ft) above sea level where traces of an ancient chapel dedicated to St Michael can be discerned. St Michael was the angel who, according to the Book of Revelations, battled with the evil dragon when there was war in heaven. Early Christians, who sought to personify the forces of good and evil, often dedicated hill and mountaintop churches to him because they believed a foundation so sited would be aptly positioned for dealing with the forces of evil which they knew surrounded them. Although there is no record of the history of the chapel, its origins stretch far back into the foggy mists of time and it is positioned where the three parishes of Llanddewi Skirrid, Llantilio Pertholey and Llanvihangel Crucor meet.

A local tradition maintains that at the exact moment that Christ died on the cross a bolt of lightning struck the summit of the mountain and split it asunder, giving it the distinct broken look that it has today. Legends such as this have helped give the mountain a mystical heritage and there was a time when Catholics would climb to the summit to hold services in the mountain chapel of St Michael. An ancient route to the summit is still used today and up this path great numbers of worshippers would struggle on Good Friday and St Michael's Day (29th September). The reverence with which the mountain was held in the local community is illustrated by the number of farmers who, even within living memory, would fill sacks of earth with soil from their 'holy' mountain and then spread it over the floors of their byres in the belief that it would protect their livestock against disease or else cure them of any ailments.

lie at the bottom of the lake, and there are several legends as to how this city was overcome by its waters.

One of the most frequently told is that a young man of the town fell in love with the daughter of the local lord only to have his advances spurned because of his poverty. Not to be so easily thwarted the lover went out and murdered her father's steward when he was returning from collecting rents from his tenants. Now, suitably wealthy, he was able to win the girl's hand and the two were duly married. But during the marriage feast a spectral voice was heard to cry *'Dial a ddaw! Dial a ddaw!'* ('Vengeance is coming!') The voice warned that tragedy would befall both the couple and their

Hidden realms of
Ancient Gods

Determined now her tomb to build
Her ample skirts with stones she filled,
And dropped a heap on Carnmore;
Then stepped one thousand yards, to Loar,
And dropped another goodly heap;
And then with one prodigious leap
Gained Carnbeg; and on its height
Displayed the wonders of her might.

JONATHAN SWIFT (1667-1745).

Ireland

Ireland's origins are shrouded in a mist so thick that they are obscured from the gaze of even the most dedicated historical researcher. The great passage tombs in the Boyne Valley, Newgrange and Knowth are decorated with

PAGE 118: *Gallarus Oratory - best visited after the tourist buses have left.*

PREVIOUS PAGE: *Glendalough, or 'the Glen of Two Lakes'.*

KEY
1. Grinan of Aileach
2. Beltany Stone Circle
3. Croagh Patrick
4. Knocknarea
5. Hill of Tara
6. Newgrange
7. Glendalough
8. Poulnabrone Dolmen
9. Gallams Oratoryr
10. Lough Gur

such exquisite lines, whorls and spirals that they are, in many ways, reminiscent of the technical skills and mathematical precision demonstrated by those behind the creation of the Egyptian pyramids. Yet they predate these acknowledged wonders by more than a thousand years. The peoples responsible for their construction are a tantalizing enigma, and their everyday lives and religious beliefs can only be guessed at.

Folklore, however, maintains that five specific groups of invaders have populated Ireland, and it is to the penultimate of these, the Tuatha de Danann (The People of the Goddess Danu), that mystical Ireland truly belongs. Having ruled the land for nine generations, this race of gods were driven out by the Milesians from whom the present-day Irish are said to be descended. However, they did not leave Ireland but instead used their magical powers to retreat into a mystical realm, where they dwelt beyond the *sidhes*, those grassy mounds and barrows that still speckle the landscape today. They became the Aes Sidhe, or 'People of the Hills' – the fairies, whose existence is an integral part of the Irish psyche.

GRIANAN OF AILEACH
NR. LETTERKENNY, COUNTY DONEGAL
An Ancient Thought Where Legends Abound
Grianan of Aileach occupies a spectacular location on top of Greenan Mountain, which at 245m (803ft) high provides fine views over loughs Swilley and Foyle, and is a truly impressive and impregnable ring-fort, or *cashel*, steeped in mystery. Its name has been translated as 'Stone Palace of the

ABOVE: *The antiquity and fame of Grianan of Aileach, the 'Stone Palace of the Sun,' is such that it was marked on a 2nd-century map of the world.*

Sun', 'Fortress of the Sun' or even 'Stone Temple of the Sun'. Although it has been heavily restored, its origins are most certainly ancient and stretch far back into the foggy mists of time. It is thought to date from around 1700 BC and has the distinction of being one of only five sites in Ireland that are marked on the Egyptian geographer Ptolemy's (c.90–168) 2nd-century map of the world.

From the 5th to the 12th centuries the fort was the stronghold of the O'Neill kings of Ulster. There is a tradition that the fort was destroyed in 1101 by Murtogh O'Brien, the ruler of Munster in retaliation for the O'Neills having destroyed his royal seat at Kincora some 13 years previously. O'Brien demanded the annihilation of his enemy's stronghold, and to ensure that it could not be rebuilt he instructed each of his soldiers to take a stone away from the fort as they left. Grianan of Aileach was finally reconstructed between 1874 and 1879 by Derry antiquarian Dr Walter Bernard, although there is some doubt about the accuracy of the interior restoration.

Whether or not the restoration is true to the original layout, there can be no doubt that the site itself is both magical and impressive. According to legend it was constructed in Ireland's ethereal past by Dagda the god-king of the mystical Tuatha de Danann to protect the grave of his murdered son Aedh. Another tradition holds that the *cashel*

was the palace of hibernation for the Celtic sun-goddess, Graine, and as such was once a place of sun worship. Whatever its original purpose, it is difficult not to be moved by this windswept place. You feel dwarfed by its mighty walls which stand 5m (17ft) high and 4m (13ft) thick, and you come away believing implicitly that this mystical place of rare beauty could only be the work of Ireland's ancient gods.

BELTANY STONE CIRCLE
NR. STABANE, COUNTY DONEGAL
Mysterious Stones in Idyllic Surroundings

A muddy climb along a rough path brings you to the exposed summit of Tops Hill, where there stands the truly enchanting stone circle of Beltany, a name derived from Baal Tinne ('the Fire of Baal'), which suggests that the pagan practice of sun worship was once carried out at this lovely spot. The circle, comprising of 64 stones but originally far larger, is sometimes referred to as 'the Stonehenge of Donegal', although archaeology dates it to around 2000 BC, making it a good 200 years older than Stonehenge.

Of course, the passage of time has obliterated any remnants of the paint or clay with which those ancient worshippers may have decorated the stones and their surroundings. Lost also are the words that would have been uttered, along with any trace of the rituals that were practiced here. There can be little doubt, however, that people came here to venerate the deity

ABOVE: *The hilltop location of the Beltany Stone Circle exudes an aura that is both breathtaking and spiritual.*

Baal, the great sun-god and ruler of nature. These celebrations were always carried out on a hilltop so as to ensure a view of the rising sun at the exact moment that it began its climb into the sky. Tradition holds that the principal ceremonies were held on 21st June, on which day the lawgivers lit sacred fires at the centre of the circle, symbolizing the sun, while the surrounding stones represented the stars.

This is a truly mystical location and a genuine aura of magic and sacredness pervades the whole site. Indeed, as you begin the trudge back down the hillside you are left with the overwhelming sensation that your visit has re-energized you, and that you have shared the same sense of awe and wonder that people must have felt when they came here to worship long, long ago.

CROAGH PATRICK
COUNTY MAYO
Where St Patrick Faced Ireland's Demons

The looming bulk of Croagh Patrick, which is also known as 'The Reek' and rises to a height of 765m (2,510ft), is Ireland's sacred mountain, and has been since long before St Patrick walked its mysterious slopes. Indeed, archaeological evidence suggests that people have been climbing this conical mountain to commune with their gods for perhaps 5,000 years. To the Celtic peoples of Ireland it was the dwelling place of their deity Crom Dubh and the principal site of their harvest festival of Lughnasa, which was traditionally held around 1st August.

According to Christian tradition, St Patrick came to the hallowed mountain during Lent in AD 441 and spent 40 days and nights in prayer and contemplation. He was forced to overcome all manner of temptations and demonic interference. It was during his time on the mountain that he summoned forth a host of abhorrent and venomous creatures, and ordered them to cast themselves over the edge of the mountain. Tradition holds that today's absence of snakes in Ireland is the result of St Patrick's antics on the scree-strewn slopes of the holy mountain.

St Patrick succeeded in overcoming the old religion, and Christianity stamped its own beliefs onto this mysterious mountain which looks down onto the blue waters of Clew Bay below. By the 7th century Croagh Patrick had become one of the two most important Christian places of pilgrimage in Ireland. Originally, pilgrimages to the mountain's top were made in Lent, but following a ferocious tempest that caused the deaths of 30 pilgrims in 1113, the date for the processions to the summit was changed to summer, with the most popular days being the last Friday and Sunday of July.

Today, nearly one million pilgrims a year follow in St Patrick's footsteps and make the exhausting climb up the mountain. Their feet have worn a rutted path that winds its way along the spine and climbs steeply to the summit, where the faithful can kneel in prayer and renounce evil, just as St Patrick did. Many undertake the ascent barefooted as an act of penance for their wrongdoings, while some even struggle up the harsh slopes on their knees. Traditionally, the last Sunday in July is always the busiest day on the mountain and as many as 40,000 people carrying traditional blackthorn sticks make their way to the oratory on the windswept summit. There they circle the little chapel and the place where the saint is said to have made his bed, saying the rosary whilst petitioning him for special favours. In so doing they are merely following a custom that predates Christianity and which stretches back over thousands of years to a time when the ancient inhabitants of Ireland came to this same summit to celebrate life's abundance during their festival of Lughnasa.

KNOCKNAREA
Nr. Standhill, County Sligo
A Legendary Queen's Hilltop Tomb

Knocknarea, 'Hill of the Moon' or 'Hill of the Kings', is a truly striking landmark that dominates Sligo Bay and the Coolera peninsula. On its windswept summit there stands one of the most impressively situated cairns in the whole of Britain and Ireland, a flat-topped dome made up of thousands of small stones and rounded boulders that has long been revered as the legendary burial place of Maeve, the Iron Age Queen of Connacht. It is even said she was interred at the centre of the mound standing upright, a warrior-queen to the last.

Legends aside, the proportions of the cairn are truly impressive. It rises from a base 55m (180 ft) across to a height of 10m (32ft), and it has been calculated that the small stones from which it is constructed weigh in the region of 40,000 tons, which would have made it a colossal undertaking and must mean that it was intended to propagate the memory of a person or event of stupendous significance. It was most probably built by Neolithic peoples about 3000 BC and the likelihood is that it does cover a passage tomb.

What is most intriguing about Miosgan Meadhbha ('The Grave of Maeve') is that it has never been excavated or even violated since the day it was sealed some 5,000 years ago, and so nobody knows for certain what lies at its heart. Its size is supposed to increase with every visitor to the summit, since tradition calls for each climber to bring and add a stone to the cairn. Of course modern technology has infiltrated these parts and a popular pastime of many who today trudge their

BELOW: *Be sure to take a boulder with you when you ascend Knocknarea Hill in County Sligo, in order that you can add to Queen Maeve's tomb.*

way up Knocknarea's unyielding slopes, is to stand panting and breathless on the top of the cairn, whip out their mobile phones and dial up friends, family or colleagues to boast of their achievement!

THE HILL OF TARA
COUNTY MEATH
Ireland's Seat of Kings

Tara Hill was one of the most revered religious sites in early Ireland, and was the seat of the Irish High Kings from the 3rd to the 11th centuries. Yet the casual visitor may at first glance be somewhat disappointed at what they find here. No crumbling ruin crowns its summit, no tangible signs of its regal past survive, save simple earthworks. Yet it is a magical place, steeped in history and legend, and to stride across its gentle slopes is to follow in the footsteps of gods and kings, saints and heroes.

A large number of monuments and earthen structures are scattered over the hill. The oldest and most prominent of these is the Mound of the Hostages, which is a Megalithic passage tomb constructed in or around 2500 BC. The name 'Mound of the Hostages' derives from the custom of over-

kings, such as those at Tara, of retaining important personages from subject kingdoms to ensure their submission. Aligned to it is the so-called Banqueting Hall, a name used in medieval literature which wrongly recognized it as the place where thousands of guests enjoyed banquets and the *feis*, those great national assemblies that took place every three years and at which laws were passed, tribal differences settled and the defence of the realm decided. There is a suggestion that this Neolithic earthwork may possibly have been the ceremonial entrance to the Hill on which all the major roads of ancient Ireland converged, but this is little more than speculation.

To the south of the Mound of the Hostages, inside the bank and the ditch of the so-called Royal Enclosure, stand two linked ring-forts, one of which is known as the Forradh. At its centre lies the Lia Fáil, the Stone of Destiny. According to legend this magical stone was brought to Tara by the Tuatha de Danann. It was once Ireland's coronation stone, over which monarchs were crowned and which was said to emit a fearsome roar of recognition when touched by the rightful king of Tara.

The stone has stood on the hill since the times when magnificent wooden palaces dominated the brow. Its memories are Ireland's memories of ancient glories and long-ago kings. It has witnessed the huge crowds that flocked here to enjoy great banquets, while being entertained by athletes, combatants, poets, musicians, minstrels and jesters. It warmed to the glow of firelight as storytellers gathered their audiences around them and, using nothing but the magic of the spoken voice, spirited them away into the realm of the gods, where they held them spellbound with breathless tales of ancient conflicts and heroic conquests. Tales such as that of the mighty warrior Lugh of the Long Hand, who came here to lead the mystical Tuatha de Danann into battle against their enemies the evil Fomorians. A warrior such as he had never been seen in Ireland before, and so bright was the radiance of his countenance that when he stood upon Tara's heights people thought the sun had risen in the west. He wore the Milky Way as a silver chain around his neck, had a rainbow for his sling, and possessed a sword called 'The Answerer' with which he could cleave through both walls and armour. Before riding into battle at the head of a great host of warriors, he equipped himself with every magical weapon known to the world. His forces inflicted a crushing defeat upon the Fomorians and banished them from Ireland forever, after which the Tuatha de Danann returned to Tara and ruled for nine generations, until the arrival from Spain of the Milesians, ancestors of the modern Irish.

These were the sagas and oral histories with which the

LEFT: *The Hill of Tara is one of the most spiritually charged and sacred locations in the whole of Ireland.*

ABOVE: *Although the exact function of Ireland's most ancient site, Newgrange, is unknown, it is without doubt a sophisticated leftover from the days of an ancient culture.*

storytellers would regale their audiences in the halls of Tara. Of how with the coming of the Milesians the history of modern Ireland began. How at Kenmare Bay in County Kerry the two sides fought a battle during which the de Danann queen, Eriu, was fatally wounded, but before she died she made the Milesian leader, Amorgen, promise that the island would bear her name forever and thus it became Eriu, Eire or Eireann.

As the epic tales approached their climax, the audiences would have listened with baited breath to the story of the final confrontation between the two forces on the Plain of Teltown, to the north of Tara. Of how the invaders finally overwhelmed the Tuatha de Danann who, rather than be exiled from their land, used their magical powers to retreat into a mystical realm, leaving Ireland to their conquerors. Thereafter, they dwelt beyond the *sidhes*, those grassy mounds and barrows that speckle the landscape of Ireland to this day. They became, according to the storytellers, the Aes Sidhe, or 'People of the Hills', the fairies whose existence has become rooted in the Irish psyche and whose mysterious otherworld has provided a final refuge in times of trouble. Every god was a Fer-Sidhe, or 'man of the hill', and every goddess a Bean-Sidhe, or 'woman of the hill' – the *banshee* of popular Irish legend.

Ages went by, many kings were crowned over the Stone of Destiny, living and dying at Tara. At some time around AD 430 Loegaire became the 116th king and it was during his reign that the Christian God arrived on Tara's slopes in the robust form of St Patrick. He challenged the pagan powers by lighting a Pascal fire on the nearby Hill of Slane. The Druid Priests warned Loegaire that, if he did not extinguish the fire immediately it would burn in Ireland forever. But the king ignored their warnings and St Patrick came to Tara. He plucked a shamrock from the hillside and used its three leaves and single stem to teach Loegaire about the nature of the Trinity. Thus it was that Christianity came to Ireland and the emblem of the nation was born. It was this new faith that, ultimately, sounded Tara's death-knell. According to legend, King Diarmaid, who ascended the throne in 558, arrested and executed the murderer of a tax collector who had taken sanctuary with St Ruadhan. Incensed by Diarmaid's actions, the saint came to Tara and, ringing his

a thin pencil of light is guided inside to creep across the floor of the chamber. As the light widens, the dark ancient tomb becomes dramatically illuminated and the effect is pure magic as past, present and future seem to blend harmoniously. After around 14 short minutes the light retreats back down the passage, and the spell is suddenly broken as the heart of Newgrange is plunged once more into darkness.

This annual miracle is the most heralded event in the Irish cultural calendar, and yet very little is known about the pagan engineers who constructed the massive stone dome more than 5,000 years ago. It is believed that they placed the narrow entrance at the exact point where it could capture the first glint of the sunrise on the shortest day of the year in order that its rays would

sacred bell, pronounced the fateful incantation 'Desolate be Tara for ever and ever'. Soon after, the palace lay abandoned and its buildings were left to rot with only the Stone of Destiny remaining as a witness to the ending of its glories.

All is quiet here now. The heroes have departed. The ashes of the fires by whose glowing logs the storytellers once wove their magic have long since been raked into the hillside. The fairy folk have retreated ever further into their secret, enchanted domain. But it is still possible in a quiet moment to stand upon Tara's heights and, with the breeze upon your face, connect with the true spirit of the place. 'If you go there,' wrote the poet Francis Ledwidge from the mud-spattered trenches of Flanders, 'look all around you and remember me to every hill and wood and ruin, for my heart is there. Say I will come back again surely, and maybe you will hear pipes in the grass or a fairy horn – I have heard them often from Tara.'

NEWGRANGE
COUNTY MEATH
Long Ago Tribute Where the Sun still Shines

The passage grave of Newgrange is one of Ireland's most ancient and numinous sites. It is a place where on the winter solstice (21st December) it becomes possible to witness an impressive example of ancient astronomy at work. As dawn heralds the end of the longest night of the year, the sun begins to rise over the Boyne Valley. Suddenly its warming rays touch the roof-box over the entrance of Newgrange, and

shine upon the ashes of their dead, deep within the tomb, and that it was also intended as a sign of rebirth, marking the point when the changing of the season brought renewed life to their crops and animals.

Newgrange was originally built around 3100 BC, and is the largest of the Neolithic passage tombs that cluster around the Boyne Valley. The main structure of Newgrange was surrounded by standing stones, only 12 of which are still standing. The passage tomb itself is constructed of granite quarried from the Mourne Mountains to the north, and of dazzling white quartz from the Wicklow Mountains. The effect is striking against the green countryside. The journeys to acquire these resources would have been both time-consuming and dangerous, so it is more than apparent that white quartz and granite held great significance to the builders of Newgrange. In addition the construction depended on a very precise engineering capability in order for the roof to stay in place, since no mortar was used in its construction.

Yet the exact function of Newgrange remains a mystery. There is a general consensus that it was intended as a burial mound, although another theory holds that it was also used as a temple for sun worship, hence its alignment with the rising sun of the winter solstice. Interestingly, the white quartz was only used on the eastern side of the mound which faces the sun. Other evidence for sun-worshipping builders is the beautiful artwork found etched into the stones throughout the structure. The complex patterns of loops, spirals, diamonds and zigzags have been interpreted as symbols for the sun. It has been pointed out that an essentially agricultural community would have benefited enormously from a device to mark the point in the year when the winter turned, and with the days beginning to grow longer the cycle of planting and harvesting could begin again.

Of course, inevitably, all such theories are little more than speculation and the true purpose of this remarkable place may never be known. Yet to the thousands of visitors who come to this place of ancient mystery, or the fortunate few whose names are drawn in the annual lottery to enter the chamber at dawn on the winter solstice, explanations are unnecessary. All that needs to be understood is that this is a sacred place imbued with the beliefs and spirituality of an ancient culture.

GLENDALOUGH
COUNTY WICKLOW
The Holy Glen

Glendalough or 'the Glen of Two Lakes' is a truly enchanting place where an ancient ecclesiastical settlement nestles beneath the cliffs of a tranquil valley. An ideal spot in which to enjoy a few moments of quiet contemplation, while exploring the delights of one of the most important monastic ruins in Ireland. In the 6th century this hidden-away glen would have been a desolate and isolated spot, and as such made the perfect place for St Kevin to build his hermitage, once he had decided to foresake the fertile lands of County Kildare and withdraw into a simple life of prayer

and meditation amidst the solitude of the thinly populated Wicklow Mountains.

At first he settled into a small cave that can still be seen 30 feet above the upper of Glendalough's two lakes. Now known as St Kevin's Bed this little cave measures just four feet wide by three feet high, and is probably one of the oldest man-made relics in the glen. It may well have originally been a rock-cut tomb dating from around 2000 BC, but today it is inextricably linked with the life and legends of St Kevin. According to one story, temptation pursued him in the form of a lustful woman who arrived at the saintly hermit's cave intent on seducing him. St Kevin was not about to give up on his vow of chastity and so resorted to the decisively effective, though extremely unholy, defence, of hurling her over the cliff and into the lake beneath! Another version has it that he discouraged her by throwing nettles in her face, whereupon she apologized to him and thereafter dedicated herself to a life of piety.

Whether or not the legend of the attempted seduction is true, St Kevin's reputation and chastity survived intact. By the time he died in AD 617, at the ripe old age of 120, many

OPPOSITE: *Legend has it that St Kevin, the monk who built Glendalough monastery, was also a murderer.*

BELOW: *The Poulnabrone Dolmen stands amidst the almost lunar landscape of the Burren and is one of the most photographed monuments in Ireland.*

disciples had flocked to his settlement and he had established a thriving community in this little slice of paradise high up in the Wicklow Mountains.

Over the centuries that followed Glendalough grew into one of the most famous centres of Christianity in Ireland and was renowned as a seat of learning throughout Europe. Viking raids from the 9th century onwards did a lot of damage to the settlement, and there was a disastrous fire in 1398 which caused the settlement to decline. It was finally destroyed in the 16th century and today only a handful of buildings, several of them in ruin, survive to attest to what a magnificent and holy place it once was.

The surviving buildings include the well-preserved St Kevin's Church, which is a one-roomed structure that is also known as St Kevin's Kitchen. There are the remains of seven churches scattered around the site. But without doubt Glendalough's chief glory is its splendid Round Tower, which dates from the 10th century. Some 33.5m (110ft) high it would have been used as a bell tower to call pilgrims from afar. At other times it was a place of refuge for the community whenever the area was under attack. That is why the door is located about a third of the way up the tower and could only be reached by a ladder, which would be pulled up to stop undesirables being able to gain entrance. Although it was recapped in 1876, the main body of the Glendalough Round Tower is still in almost perfect condition even though it has withstood the ravages of almost 1,000 years.

POULNABRONE DOLMEN
Nr. Kilfenora, County Clare
A Little Slice of Ancient Ireland
The Burren sweeps inland from the jagged cliffs of Ireland's Atlantic coastline and is a forlornly desolate terrain of grey, weathered limestone slabs, devoid of trees and shrubs. It is littered with the remnants of early settlers who somehow managed to eke out a living from its bleak lunar-like landscape. Chief amongst these remnants is the Poulnabrone Dolmen, a truly impressive portal tomb that dates from around 3600 BC, and which today is said to be the most photographed prehistoric monument in Ireland. Its thin capstone appears to balance precariously on two portal stones that give the appearance of having sprouted from the limestone pavement.

The eastern portal stone was replaced in 1985, following the alarming discovery that it had cracked. Excavations at the time uncovered the uncremated bones of between 16 and 22 adults, six juveniles and one newborn baby. Only one of the adults had lived beyond 40 years, and the majority were under 30 when they died. It was proved that the bones had actually been de-fleshed elsewhere, probably by burying them at another location, then digging them up and transferring the bones into the dolmen. The fact that the burials appear to have been spread over a period of 600 years suggests that this may have been a ceremonial cemetery for important individuals. It may also have been the focus of religious ceremonies at certain times of the year which had particular significance to a farming group, such as spring and autumn.

The Poulnabrone Dolmen exudes an air of mysterious enchantment, and its austere simplicity, set against the almost bizarre backcloth of the Burren's stark topography, exudes a strange and awesome power. You can easily picture those ancient people lovingly laying their dead to rest, and returning to perform their rituals and services as they attempted to contact the spirits of their relatives, possibly asking them to intervene with the gods to ensure the fertility of their crops on this barren, inhospitable and uncertain landscape. Here in a quiet moment it is still possible to sense something of the magic that those long-ago peoples must have felt. But then another coach load of visitors arrive, the cameras click and the sense of connection slips away.

GALLARUS ORATORY
Dingle Peninsula, County Kerry
A Holy Place Where Time Stands Still
The rolling mountains and sea breezes of the Dingle Peninsula can often hide a rich archaeological past from the visitor. Of the many heritage sites on the peninsula Gallarus Oratory is unique in both its setting and mystique. Situated on natural farmland and exposed to the wild Atlantic winds and weather, this lovely little building of stone without mortar resembles an upturned boat. The fact that it is still waterproof clearly demonstrates the skills of the humble ecclesiastical craftsmen who constructed it 1,200 years ago. It is the oldest intact building in Ireland, and it was built for prayer at a time when the world was universally thought to be charged with the active spirit of a personal God.

Once inside this masterpiece of ancient stonework you are enveloped by the spirit of the past as your imagination soars back to an ancient era when the surrounding countryside – eerily beautiful, yet frighteningly hostile and isolated – acted as a magnet to those who came in search of contemplative solitude. Here, perched on the edge of Europe, or as they saw it the edge of eternity, monks and hermits could seek their God in a raw, ecstatic encounter with stone, wind, sea and sky.

Today, the age of miracles has given way to the age of science, and universal materialism has brought a strange paradox to this sacred place of spiritual simplicity. Bus loads

OPPOSITE: *Stand alone inside Dingle's Gallarus Oratory when the tour buses have departed and the ambience of a bygone and holy age takes hold of your senses.*

of camera-wielding tourists 'doing Ireland' make up the largest proportion of its visitors. They traipse obediently through the visitors' centre, walk the grass path that meanders up to the tiny Oratory, pose for a few digital pictures, walk back to their buses and are gone. Yet in a quiet moment in the early morning or late evening, when the tour buses have parked up for the night, it is possible to stand alone within this ancient structure and listen to the Atlantic winds flinging themselves with demented fury against the stone walls. Then the Oratory appears to shiver wearily as it braces itself against another onslaught. At these moments you can sense the presence of those men of God to whom life was but a fleeting moment in which to prepare for that which lies beyond.

LOUGH GUR, NR. HOLYCROSS
COUNTY LIMERICK
The Sacred Lough

Cradled by the embrace of a circle of low-lying hills that keep the outside world firmly at bay, the glassy, grey waters of Lough Gur have long been regarded as a sacred otherworld, the haunted preserve of fairies, gods and legendary heroes.

'Lough Gur is enchanted,' wrote David Fitzgerald in his 1879 *Popular Tales of Ireland*, '… in the past, no minstrel, piper, or poet would willingly spend a night within a mile of its shore, such was its fearful reputation and potency. Even to fall asleep in daytime on its banks was considered among them to be reckless folly.'

Tradition places Lough Gur under the aegis of Aine, the fairy love-goddess who was believed to tempt mortals into acts of passion. Maurice Fitzgerald, the first earl of Desmond, is said to have one day encountered her in the Lough. Having taken her cloak, an action that magically placed her under his power, he was able to lay with her and thus was born an enchanted son, Geroid Iarla. Maurice raised the boy at his castle on the shores of Lough Gur, but Aine warned him that if he ever showed surprise at anything their son did, then the boy would be compelled to return to her world.

As a young man Geroid showed great promise in the art of poetry, and is said to have been able to compose 'witty and ingenious' verses in Gaelic. He also excelled in magic as befitting one who was half a god. One day (some say it was in 1398), during a banquet at his father's castle, Geroid became involved in a competition of magical prowess with a young woman. Determined to surpass her skills, Geroid leapt in and out of a tiny bottle. On seeing his son perform such an impossible feat, Maurice let out a cry of impressed astonishment. Suddenly, a cold breeze blew through the hall and Geroid left the feast and walked slowly to the shores of the lake. Turning to wave farewell to his father, he went into its waters and, as he did so, was transformed into a goose. His heartbroken father watched as the bird drifted toward Garrett Island, where it slowly faded into nothingness.

When the waters of the Lough are tranquil and still, it is said that Geroid Iarla's enchanted castle is occasionally glimpsed deep beneath the surface. Here he lives waiting for the day when he can return to the world of mortals. Once every seven years, when a full moon bathes the lough in its eerie hue, he emerges from its depths riding a white horse and leads a fairy cavalcade onto the land where, having encircled the shores, they dance their way back into the lake.

Lough Gur is a special place that has been sacred to those who have lived upon its magical shores since long before Christianity came to Ireland. The rich abundance of well-preserved cromlechs, dolmens, tumuli and other archaeological treasures scattered about its shores and surrounding countryside proudly announce its mystical past. To come here in the silence of an early morning, when the sun's first rays sparkle upon its surface, and the breezes fresh with the scent of the new day, you may be forgiven for thinking that gods and fairies truly do walk amongst us.

LEFT: *Lough Gur in County Limerick is Ireland's sacred lake, an otherworldly preserve of the gods, fairies and legendary heroes.*

Windswept Region of Ancient Mystery

✴

Angel, spirits of sleep,
White-robed, with silver hair,
In your meadows fair,
Where the willows weep,
And the sad moonbeam
On the gliding stream
Writes her scatter'd dream:

FROM 'SPIRITS'
BY ROBERT BRIDGES (1844-1930).

Northumberland, Cumbria Durham & Yorkshire

From the urban spread of industrial Lancashire, through the magical and awesome scenery of the Lake District, the tranquil enchantment of Yorkshire to the wild and untamed Northumberland coast, the North of England comprises an area that revels in a stunning abundance of scenic delights. To this area came the Romans and several of

PAGE 132: *Benwell Roman Temple is the only known British temple that is dedicated to the god Antenociticus, who may have been a local Celtic deity.*

PREVIOUS PAGE: *Fountains Abbey is still a great source of inspiration and awe.*

KEY
1. Holy Island
2. Lady's Well
3. Castlerigg Stone Castle
4. Long Meg
5. Benwell Roman Temple
6. Durham Cathedral
7. Whitby Abbey
8. Fountains Abbey
9. All Saints Church

ABOVE: *Lindisfarne, or Holy Island, was once the centre of Christianity in Britain. It can only be reached at low tide, across a three-mile causeway.*

their surviving temples reflect how they were willing to assimilate the native deities into their own beliefs. On the north-east coast in the 7th century a golden age held sway as the likes of St Aidan and St Cuthbert brought Christianity to the ancient kingdom of Northumberland. In the 8th century, Viking raiders brought terror to the north-west coast. As they moved inland and began to settle they brought with them tales of dragons, ogres, trolls and demon hounds, and transplanted these fearsome creatures into the dark places that Celtic legend had already imbued with an evil reputation. Their descendants would become the cattle-stealers and ferocious warlords who ravaged and pillaged the Scottish borderlands throughout the Middle Ages. The consequence of this rich mixture of so many different cultures is today evident in the wonderful array of sacred sites that are scattered across this inspiring landscape.

HOLY ISLAND
NORTHUMBERLAND
The Golden Age

The 7th century was the golden age for the Anglo-Saxon kingdom of Northumbria, which stretched from the Humber to the Forth. Its capital was Bamburgh where the castle of the Northumbrian kings, on its massive whinstone crag, gazed across the sea to Lindisfarne, the Holy Island from which Christianity was spread throughout the region. In 635 King Oswald summoned Aidan to Bamburgh from the saintly island of Iona, and charged him with the task of converting his subjects to Christianity. Perhaps it was its similarity to Iona that led Aidan to base himself on the island of Lindisfarne. From here Aidan went forth and preached his message throughout Oswald's realm. A vivid testimony to his success can still be seen at Lindisfarne Priory where, on a Saxon tombstone, the Northumbrians are shown on one side fighting with battle-axes, and on the other kneeling in adoration before the Cross.

In 642 Oswald was slain in battle by Penda of Mercia when he besieged Bamburgh. Penda championed the pagan gods and was determined to force the old religion back upon the people of Northumbria. From Lindisfarne Aidan watched as Penda stacked piles of wood against the castle walls, obviously intending to burn it down. 'See, Lord,' he prayed, 'what ill Penda worketh.' Suddenly the wind changed direction, blowing clouds of smoke and fire into the faces of the would-be attackers and the castle was saved.

It is, however, with St Cuthbert, who came to the island in 665, that Lindisfarne is most closely identified. He worked on the island for 12 years and was much loved and respected by the monks. Then, wishing to further dedicate himself to a life of prayer, he withdrew alone to the Farne Islands and, on the one that now bears his name, lived as a hermit for nine years, during which time his sanctity became famous throughout Europe. He returned in 685 to assume the Bishopric of Lindisfarne but two years later, worn out by a life of self-mortification, he died and was buried in the priory church, where his body became one of the monks most treasured possessions. The monastery soon became famed as one of the greatest centres of art and learning in Europe, and the monks lived contented in secure piety, dedicating themselves to creating items of stunning craftsmanship, such as the exquisitely beautiful Lindisfarne Gospels.

This golden age of Christian culture ended abruptly with the coming of the Vikings. In 793, according to the *Anglo-Saxon Chronicle* 'terrible portents appeared over Northumbria… and a little while after that the harrying of the heathen miserably destroyed God's church in Lindisfarne.' When in 875 the Danes ravaged the island for a second time, the monks took flight carrying with them the body of St Cuthbert and, in the same coffin, the head of the man who had first brought missionaries to Northumbria, St Oswald. For over a century the holy relics were moved from place to place, once even returning to Lindisfarne for a year, until they found a permanent resting place in Durham Cathedral.

Nothing now remains of the Saxon church and monastery on Lindisfarne, save fragments of stone and grave slabs. The ruins of the Benedictine priory, the massive sandstone pillars and graceful arches which totter close to the wild shoreline, date to the 12th century.

The island itself can only be reached at low tide, via a three-mile causeway that twists across an almost forlorn wilderness of shimmering mud flats and delivers you to what is still a sacred and magical place where the alchemy of sky and sea serve to obliterate virtually all the stresses and worries of the modern world.

BELOW: The *Lady's Well in Holystone is now a tranquil place, perfect for quiet contemplation.*

LADY'S WELL
HOLYSTONE, NORTHUMBERLAND
The Lady's Well

The tiny village of Holystone nestles on a tranquil stretch of the River Coquet amidst a beautiful myth-drenched landscape of magical springs, glorious waterfalls and stunning scenery. In the Middle Ages a convent dedicated to the Virgin Mary stood here, and although the foundation was never a rich one (it was worth only £11 at the time of its dissolution) the nuns tended a well that even then had an ancient pedigree and had long been designated as a sacred and holy place. Nothing of the nunnery survives today, but the picturesque pool which the sisters christened the 'Lady's Well' still sits serenely in a quiet field surrounded by a grove of tall trees, the reflections of which shimmer ghost-like in its rippling waters. The pond was once known as 'Ninian's Well' based on the belief that St Ninian, Bishop of Whithorn in south-west Scotland between 500 and 550, once came to the site, although there is no real evidence to suggest that he ever did.

It is difficult to imagine that this peaceful little spot was once a thriving place of pilgrimage, to which crowds flocked in their thousands. Over Easter 627, Paulinus, an early Christian missionary, is said to have baptized 3,000 converts, including the Northumbrian king, Edwin, at the well. As a result the pool has also been known as 'St Paulinus Well' and a statue of the saint was placed at the centre of the pool in

ABOVE: *Castlerigg Stone Circle is over 5,000 years old. Its purpose is not clear, although some think that it might be an astronomical observatory.*

the 1780s when the stone tank that now holds the water was constructed. In the 19th century that statue was replaced by the wheel cross that today makes a contemplative centrepiece for this holy place of peaceful solitude. There is a local tradition that an altar-shaped stone near the well is the 'holy' stone that gave the village its name.

CASTLERIGG STONE CIRCLE
NR. KESWICK, CUMBRIA
A Brooding Circle of Ancient Mystery

Castlerigg Stone Circle is one of the most visually impressive prehistoric monuments in Britain. It enjoys a dramatic location on high moorland and is surrounded by a sullen circle of rugged hills whose mood and appearance are as changeable as the mercurial Lakeland weather.

The circle probably dates from around 3200 BC and evidence suggests that it originally consisted of 41 stones, although only 38 now survive at the site. Some of them have long since fallen flat, although an amazing number are still standing upright. Given that they have spent some 5,000 years on the exposed moor this is little short of miraculous. All of them are unhewn boulders, some of which are over 1.5m (5ft) tall, and they all generate an aura of brooding

mystery. There is a wide opening at the circle's northern end on either side of which are two large boulders, suggesting that this may have been intended as an entrance to the site. A rectangular enclosure consisting of ten stones, and which is known as 'the cove', is situated just inside the eastern side. The original purpose of this is unknown, although excavations carried out in 1882 revealed quantities of charcoal which may have been left over from rituals.

Some hold the view that Castlerigg was used as an astronomical observatory, and some of the stones are certainly astronomically aligned, although there is no evidence that its builders ever used it as an observatory. Equally, it has been observed how several of the stones seem to reflect features of the surrounding hills, as though mirroring the landscape around them.

Whatever its original function the Castlerigg stone circle is a truly special and breathtaking place, and the combination of windswept hills and brooding solitude that hang heavy over the site provide the perfect location to ponder the beliefs and lives of our far from primitive ancestors.

LONG MEG AND HER DAUGHTERS
NR. GLASSONBY, CUMBRIA
The Stern Stone Matriarch

The remoteness of the location coupled with the eerie bleakness of the surrounding hills lend this, the third largest stone circle in England after Avebury and Stanton Drew, an aura of timeless mystery. Long Meg herself is a 3.6m (12ft) high block of red sandstone that stands 72m (238ft) to the south-west of the main circle, which consists of 59 grey stones over which Meg appears to keep a stern watch. Faint traces of spiral and ring carvings are discernible on her north-east face, and since these are reminiscent of the Bronze Age (*c.*2000–900 BC) it is possible that Meg was positioned before her daughters at some time around 2500–2000 BC.

According to legend, Meg and her daughters were a coven of 13th-century witches turned to stone by the renowned medieval wizard, Michael Scott. Here on this desolate plateau the petrified sisterhood are condemned to stand until the day dawns when someone succeeds in counting the same number of stones twice. Only then will the spell be broken and the unfortunate witches be returned to human form.

Those who might consider damaging or mistreating either Meg or her daughters should heed the fate of the 18th-century farmer, whose attempts to remove them conjured up such a ferocious and terrible storm that he thought better of it and, wisely, desisted. Similar traditions surround many of

LEFT: *Like a stern, stone matriarch the standing stone known as Long Meg dominates her nearby daughters.*

the stone circles that dot the landscapes of Britain and Ireland. However, one legend is unique to this particular site, for it is said that Meg will begin to bleed should anyone damage her or attempt to pull her down.

BENWELL ROMAN TEMPLE
Nr. Newcastle upon Tyne
Celtic Gods Meet Roman Gods

A modern housing estate provides an unlikely surrounding for this Roman temple that dates from the 2nd century AD which was dedicated to the god Antenociticus. This is the only known temple dedicated to him in Britain, and since no continental altar stones show depictions of him or inscriptions to him, it has been deduced that he may well have been a local Celtic deity who was adopted by the legionaries that were stationed at the nearby Benwell Fort. The Romans were happy to allow many different cults and religions to flourish, and the legionaries, many of whom may well have been Celts themselves, are known to have been drawn to a range of local deities. In turn the Roman soldiers passed on the Roman partiality for carved stone depictions of their gods. During excavations at the site in 1862, a head of Antenociticus was found which shows him with curly hair, two locks of which are from the crown of his head and which may have been intended to represent stags antlers. Three altars dedicated to Antenociticus by serving officers of the Roman army were also found at the site, one of whom, Tineius Longus, thanks Antenociticus for helping with his promotion to quaestor, thus suggesting that the Romans set great store in the powers of this Celtic god.

THE SANCTUARY KNOCKER
Durham Cathedral
Sanctuary, Sanctuary

Durham must surely be one of the most attractive cities in Britian, and its cathedral, begun in 1093 by Bishop William of Calais, is generally regarded as one of the outstanding examples of a Norman cathedral in Europe. It stands on the site of the Old White Church which had been built to house the remains of St Cuthbert (634–687), whose body originally lay on the island of Lindisfarne, but who was forced to undertake a period of extensive posthumous travel because of the activities of Viking raiding parties.

A far more elaborate shrine was constructed for him when the cathedral was built, and the grooves worn into the floor by the feet of innumerable pilgrims who came to shuffle past his tomb are still visible today. The list of supposed treasures that were brought to St Cuthbert's shrine included part of the rod of Moses and a piece of the manger in which the infant Jesus had lain. However, with the Dissolution of the Monasteries (1536–1540) these treasures were handed over to the Crown, and the tomb itself was

ABOVE: *Carvings such as this adorn the only known Roman temple to the god Antenociticus, who may well have been a local Celtic deity adopted by the Romans.*

opened. Reputedly, Cuthbert's body was found to be 'whole incorrupt, with his face bare and his beard as it had been a fortnight's growth.' Although the shrine was destroyed, his remains were reburied under a marble slab behind the high altar.

On the south side of the cathedral's Galilee Chapel is the tomb of the Venerable Bede (c.673-735) a notable scholar who wrote the first history of England, *The Ecclesiastical History of the English People*. As with St Cuthbert his remains were reinterred at Durham, and a magnificent shrine constructed around them. This too was broken up during the Dissolution and he now lies beneath a simple black tombstone which records simply: 'In this tomb are the bones of the Venerable Bede.'

Durham Cathedral can boast many curiosities and points of interest. It was, for example, the first church to use ribbed vaulting on a large scale. Perhaps one of its most curious artefacts is the bronze Sanctuary Knocker on its North

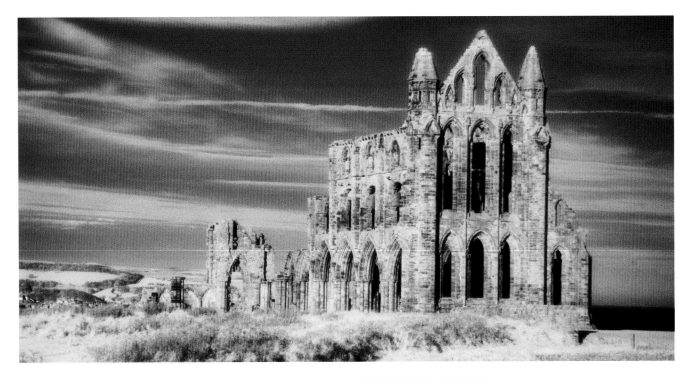

ABOVE: *The ruins of Whitby Abbey soar majestically over the town of Whitby and overlook the grey North Sea.*

Door. This is a modern replica, but the original one, which dates back to 1140, can still be seen in the cathedral's museum. It was used to attract the attention of watchmen, who occupied the chamber over the door, by criminals who had come to the cathedral to seek sanctuary. The felon was given the protection of the monastery for 40 days, during which time he had to choose between a trial or voluntary exile. If he opted for the latter, then he was escorted to a port, which was normally the bishop's port at Hartlepool. He would be forced to wear a badge in the shape of the cross of St Cuthbert and made to carry a coarse wooden cross that was tied together with rope. On arrival at the port he was required to take passage on the next ship to set sail irrespective of where it was bound.

RIGHT: *Located on Durham Cathedral's North Door, the Sanctuary Knocker was used by criminals to gain entry into the Cathedral. Once admitted, the felon was given protection for 40 days.*

WHITBY ABBEY
NORTH YORKSHIRE
An Impressive Ruin

Never is the gothic splendour of Whitby Abbey so impressive, its dramatic impact so startling as on a wild and tempestuous night, when murderous gales howl in from the grey North Sea and drive raging waves in a frenzied assault against the steadfast cliffs. During such storms, the tattered remnants of the once mighty abbey seem to shudder with the onslaught, and you can almost hear the brown stone shout defiantly back at the storms, 'topple us if you can!'

Oswy, King of Northumbria founded the monastery of Streoneshalh, from which Whitby Abbey evolved, in 657. St Hilda, a member of the royal house, was appointed as its first abbess. When she arrived at the spot where the abbey was to be built, she found the whole clifftop infested with poisonous snakes, all of which she drove to the edge of the cliff and as they tumbled over sliced off their heads with her whip, causing them to curl into tiny balls. The fossil ammonites that are found on the beach beneath the abbey, and which have been incorporated into the Whitby coat of arms, are reputed to be the petrified remnants of the snakes driven to their deaths by St Hilda.

In 664 the famous Synod of Whitby was held at the monastery, and representatives of the Celtic and Roman Church came here to debate and resolve such important matters as fixing a date for Easter. Much later, in 867, the Danes sacked the monastery and it lay desolate for the next 200 years until its resurrection as a Benedictine foundation in 1074. By the end of the 12th century the magnificent abbey, the ruins of which crown the cliff-top today, had been built.

Thereafter, its history was uneventful until its dissolution in 1540, when the lead was stripped from its roofs and the bells removed, taken to the harbour and loaded onto a ship bound for London. However, no sooner had the vessel set sail than it suddenly sank and the bells have never been recovered. Legend deems it a good omen for lovers to hear

their ghostly peal, sounding from beneath the waves, on the night before Halloween.

FOUNTAINS ABBEY
NR. RIPON, NORTH YORKSHIRE
The Monks Who Sought Escape From the World
In 1130 St Bernard of Clairvaux sent a group of monks to establish a mission in England. The monks turned their attentions to the wilds of Yorkshire and in the lonely valley of the River Rye they built Rievaulx Abbey. Their example struck a chord with some of the monks at the Benedictine Abbey of St Mary's, York, whose lives seemed to them to be too full of ease when set against the austerity of the Cistercians at Rievaulx. Thus it was that 13 of the St Mary's brethren, including their prior, Richard, sought permission from their abbot to withdraw from the city in order to follow a more simplistic and ascetic lifestyle. The abbot was convinced that such an action would reflect poorly upon the reputation of his own house and so refused to accede to their

BELOW: *The beautiful remains of Fountains Abbey remind us of the dedication and resilience of long ago men of God.*

wishes. Prior Richard duly appealed to Archbishop Turstin, a close friend of St Bernard, and in October 1132 he brought his retinue to St Mary's to decide the matter once and for all.

The abbot, however, was resentful of the interference and when the archbishop arrived at the Chapter House door, he found his way barred by the abbot and a crowd of similarly aggrieved monks. When Turstin threatened their church with an interdict he was answered with shouts of 'Interdict it for a hundred years for all we care!' A riot then broke out in the course of which the monks tried to drag Prior Richard and his followers off to prison. Turstin, however, managed to intervene and went with them into the church where they remained for some time in a state of siege. When tempers calmed down, the archbishop was able to escort the seceding monks away from St Mary's. In December 1132, the monks arrived in the lonely valley of the River Skell and there in 'a place remote from all the world, uninhabited, set with thorns, amongst the hollows of the mountains and prominent rocks fit more, as it seemed, for the dens of wild beasts than for the uses of mankind,' in a place they called De Fontibus, the monks set about establishing a tiny community. Their only shelter against the harsh midwinter weather was a thatched hut 'around the stem of the great elm, their bread being provided for them by the good Archbishop.' But during the following summer a great famine fell upon the district and the monks were forced to cook and eat the leaves of the elm that gave them shelter. One day a starving beggar came to them seeking bread and the prior, stoically observing 'Let God provide for us as He will', gave him a loaf, leaving just one for the monks to share. No sooner had the beggar gone than a cart from Knaresborough laden with loaves for the monks arrived.

Their life proved harsh and after several years they appealed directly to St Bernard of Clairvaux to help them. He responded by sending to their aid a monk named Gregory to teach them how to build. But the hardship of their day-to-day existence was beginning to take its toll and they were planning to emigrate to Clairvaux when the Dean of York died and left them all his possessions. This proved a turning point and from that time the abbey grew in both strength and numbers. Within a hundred years there arose in the lonely valley the most magnificent Cistercian buildings in the whole of England.

Fountains Abbey flourished in the centuries that followed, due largely to the monks involvement in the wool trade, and by the time of its dissolution in 1539 it is estimated that they owned 600,000 acres, including lead mines and fisheries plus a great deal of agricultural land. In 1540, the abbey was sold by the crown to Sir Richard Gresham. It was later resold to Stephen Proctor who was responsible for building Fountains Hall nearby with some of the stone from the abbey. The abbey had several further

owners until in 1768 it was purchased by William Aislabie who set about preserving what had survived the upheavals of the previous centuries, and it is due to his diligence that we are able to see the beautiful ruins and the magnificent gardens today. The view of the abbey ruins in the river valley as you approach is truly breathtaking and evokes a sense of deep awe in all who see it. The abbey church survives almost to full height, along with the nave and many windows, while the magnificent vaulted cellarium, which is over 90m (300ft) long, is truly impressive.

Here in this little slice of paradise we can stand amidst the soaring arches and lofty walls and draw inspiration from those monks' example that no matter how insurmountable our problems might seem, there is little that cannot be overcome with perseverance and faith.

ALL SAINTS' CHURCH
Rudston, East Yorkshire
The Rudston Monolith

Standing an impressive 7.5m (25ft) high and all but dwarfing the adjacent church, the Rudston Monolith is the tallest standing stone in Britain. Its rain-washed bulk is thought to have stood here since 1600 BC, although its original purpose is now long forgotten. Some say that it is fertility symbol and its obviously phallic appearance might give credence to such a theory. Indeed, a local belief says that if a man touches the stone with his wedding ring on three successive nights when the moon is waxing he will become a more effective lover.

One of the paradoxes of the stone is why such a blatantly pagan symbol was allowed to remain when the church was built. Perhaps the native religion centred upon the stone had such a powerful grip on the local community that the church had little choice but to co-exist alongside it. Or maybe the stone, which tradition maintains extends as far beneath the ground as it does above, was simply too immense for the church founders to remove and so it was left as a testimony to the power that the old gods once held over the locale. Of course, the Church then had to either Christianize or demonize the monument, and several legends attest to the attempts to do just that. One story maintains that the stone simply fell from the sky one day 'killing certain desecrators of the churchyard'. Another says that the stone arrived in the churchyard when the Devil, annoyed at the building of a church on a hill that he held sacred, hurled a stone javelin at the building. Thanks, however, to divine intervention the missile was deflected and became embedded in the ground alongside the church where it remains to this day.

OPPOSITE: *The massive Rudstone monolith stands alongside All Saints' Church. Why the church authorities allowed an obviously pagan symbol to survive is a mystery.*

Ancient Kingdoms, Sacred Islands and Silent Guardians

There comes a murmur from the shore,
And in the place two fair streams are,
Drawn from the purple hills afar,
Drawn down unto the restless sea;
The hills whose flowers ne'er fed the bee,
The shore no ship has ever seen,
Still beaten by the billows green,
Whose murmur comes unceasingly
Unto the place for which I cry.

FROM 'THE NYMPH'S SONG TO HYLAS'
BY WILLIAM MORRIS (1834–1896)

SCOTLAND

Scotland's beauty is world famous. Its magnificent mountains, serene lochs, lonely glens, tumbling rivers, gentle pastures and vast wildernesses can free the mind and stir the soul of even the most jaded. It is a country of contrasts with a complex and varied past. For centuries Scotland was a divided nation and its history is spattered with the blood of countless conflicts, many of them fought

PAGE 144: *Accessing Bughead Well is an experience in itself. Visiting this relatively new discovery is well worth the effort though.*

PREVIOUS PAGE: *Doon Hill, near Aberfolyle, Perthshire, where the fairies are rumoured to have taken the life of Robert Kirk.*

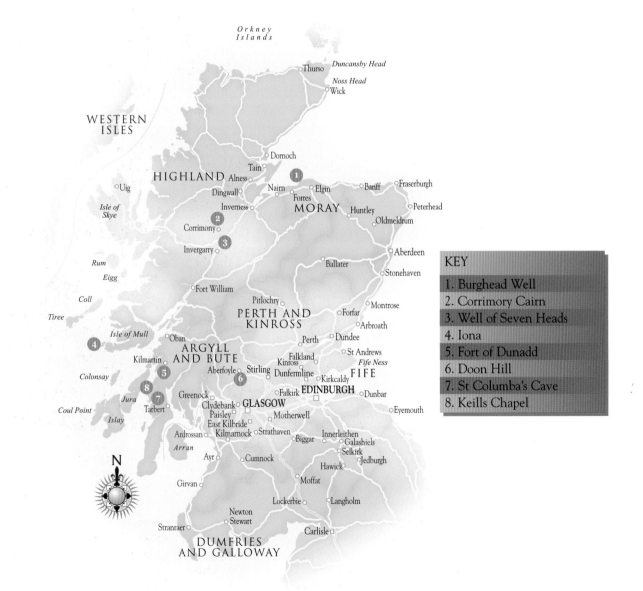

KEY
1. Burghead Well
2. Corrimory Cairn
3. Well of Seven Heads
4. Iona
5. Fort of Dunadd
6. Doon Hill
7. St Columba's Cave
8. Keills Chapel

between the Highlanders and Lowlanders. Its ethereal landscape is home to an array of heroes, giants, earth-goddesses, fearsome monsters and the wee folk, or fairies. Then there is the Island of Iona, once one of the holiest places in Christian Britain, and which remains a place that is imbued with an aura of great spirituality. Of course, Scotland was a sacred place long before the coming of Christianity. Indeed, some of the most remarkable standing stones and burial cairns in Britain are to be found dotted across its lonely moors, or standing silently in tranquil glens. So rich is Scotland in prehistoric remnants that to stand by its holy wells, or gaze across to the surrounding countryside from the lofty heights of ancient crags is to feel yourself standing amongst the gods, where anything and everything seems possible. With all this to offer, it is easy to see why Scotland is a truly magical and enchanting place to visit.

BURGHEAD WELL
BURGHEAD, MORAYSHIRE
The Dark and Enigmatic Waters
The Burghead Well is unique in Scotland. It lies beneath a curious green mound and hides behind its own high walls. To gain admittance you have to seek out the house where the key is kept, traipse back through the town and unlock the padlock of the gate that deters idle curiosity. Once through the gate you find yourself gazing at a remarkable monument, which is literally cut out of the rock. A flight of moss-covered, rough stone steps lead down into a mysterious chamber within which is a sunken, spring-fed tank. It was discovered in 1809 when what was presumed to be an old well (which was actually visible as only a slight depression in the ground) was cleared out in the hope it could act as a municipal water supply for the newly built town of Burghead. The excavations revealed the chamber and tank, and it was realized that this was a find of great historical significance. The chamber walls were repaired and the present barrel-vault entrance arch was

ABOVE: *Nobody knows for certain the origins and purpose of the Burghead Well, although the general consensus is that it was a Christian baptistery.*

added. The ancient steps were re-cut and several new ones were added. The race was now on to identify who had built this remarkable piece of ancient Scotland, as well as when they had done so and for what purpose.

At first it was believed to have been Roman, but this theory was discredited by the end of the 19th century when

the prevailing hypothesis was that the tank was in fact a Christian baptistery. In the 20th century a theory was put forward that it may well have been Celtic in origin. What was universally agreed upon, however, was that its purpose was not solely for the drawing of water, but that it was most certainly religious. Associations with water were very important in early religion. Wells, springs and the like were considered sacred and became places for worship. A Celtic stone head reputed to have been found in the Burghead Well would appear to support such a theory. Today, the general consensus is that the well is of Dark Age origin, probably Celtic, but that it was later used by early Christians as a baptistery.

Of course, its actual origins matter little. It provides us with a unique connection to the past and to the beliefs of the people who once worshipped here, be they Celtic or Christian. Its great age, together with the secrecy of its location, make it a place where you can stray down into a twilight world and reflect on and connect with the many wonders and ancient history of mystical Britain and Ireland.

ABOVE: *The curious low mound of the Corrimony Cairn affords the opportunity to crouch at the threshold between this world and the next.*

CORRIMONY CAIRN
NR. INVERNESS
An Ancient Burial Site

The passage grave of Corrimony in Glen Urquart is shielded by a line of tall trees which appear to stand guard over this curious roadside cairn that dates from before 200 BC. It consists of a rough pile of boulders formed into a circular mound, with a ring of 11 standing stones surrounding it and curious carvings can be seen on several of their surfaces. Kneeling down it is possible to squeeze your way through a narrow passage, 7m (5ft) long, and ease your way into the burial chamber, where during excavation of the cairn in 1952 traces of a human burial in a foetal position were discovered. The passage and chamber are aligned on a south-western axis, probably with some relevance to the midwinter sunset. This was an important time of rebirth in the ancient calendar, as the sun began to regain its hold over the dark nights. Squatted in this central chamber, which is now open to the elements, you really can feel as though you are on a threshold, at a place where the veil between this world and whatever lies beyond is very thin indeed. Green moss clings to its gently curving walls, and sitting there you sense the true antiquity of a place where an ambience of deep mysticism holds sway.

THE WELL OF THE SEVEN HEADS
Nr. Invergarry, Highlands
Justice was Savage

As you drive along the road that skirts the shore of Loch Oich you pass a bizarre column surmounted by seven severed stone heads, which has a particularly gory history. It all began on 25th September 1663 when Alexander MacDonald, the young Chief of Keppoch and his brother Ranald, were stabbed to death by rivals within their clan. Nothing was done to avenge their deaths until Iain Lorn, the Keppoch Bard, nagged MacDonald of Glengarry and Sir James MacDonald of Sleat to punish the criminals. Two years later, the Privy Council in Edinburgh issued letters of 'Fire and Sword' against the murderers. Another member of the Keppoch family, Ian Lom (Bald John), with the help of the MacDonalds of Sleat sought 'ample and summary vengeance' for the murders by killing and decapitating the seven murderers. It is said that on his way to Invergarry Castle, to present the heads to the chief of Clan MacDonald of Glengarry, Lom stopped at the spring to wash the heads to make them more presentable. Ever since then the spring has been known as *Tobar nan Ceann*, 'Well of the Heads'. Later, the heads were sent to Edinburgh and ordered to be 'affixit to the gallowes standing on the Gallowlie between Edinburgh and Leith'. The bodies were said to be buried in a nearby mound and have since been exhumed, thus providing evidence for the truth of the story. In 1812, the then chief of the Clan McDonell ordered the construction of the roadside obelisk to commemorate both the crime and the summary justice meted out to the perpetrators. Sitting atop the column is a sculpture of a hand holding a large dagger and around it are seven severed heads.

Although the well is most certainly not a holy well, it is interesting because the legend has parallels with the Celtic cult of head and water worship, whereby the head was taken as a trophy of success over a vanquished enemy. It also seems to show a continuation of the belief of the supposed magical properties of the severed head and water, which is a common theme in ancient mystical beliefs.

However, that aside, the well itself is neither picturesque nor particularly mysterious. You enter its chamber by a long tunnel that is somewhat claustrophobic and which this book's photographer, John Mason, summed up perfectly when he stated that 'it smells like death'.

THE ISLAND OF IONA
Iona
Scotland's Holiest Place

The tiny Isle of Iona is a mere three miles long by one mile wide, and its ancient rock is amongst the oldest on our planet, possibly dating back some 1,500 million years. It is this very ancientness that first strikes you as you glimpse its rugged shoreline from the ferry that brings you across the sound from the Island of Mull. You can sense the primeval energies crackling around you as you step ashore, and within moments of setting foot on its hallowed soil you find yourself enveloped by the mists of the past as this holiest of islands begins to weave its magic. The trials and tribulations of the modern age seem less and less important with every step you take. As the Scottish writer William Sharp, writing under the pseudonym Fiona Macleod, so eloquently put it: 'To tell the story of Iona is to go back to God, and to end in God.'

The spiritual sanctity of this little island was recognized long ago, which is proven by its old Gaelic name Innis nan Druidhneach, 'Isle of the Druids'. This mystical priesthood and their followers must have found the island a perfect refuge for the performance of their rituals. But since they have left no tangible remains we know very little about either them or their beliefs, and only a few place-names now remain to remind us of their existence.

BELOW: *The gruesome tale behind the origins of the Well of the Seven Heads may well harken back to Celtic traditions of head worship.*

Iona's modern reputation as a holy and spiritual place began in AD 563 when St Columba, together with 12 disciples, set foot on its rocky shoreline and established a religious community that would ultimately take the Christian message across Scotland and on into much of northern England.

Columcille (Columba's Irish name, meaning 'Dove of the Church') was born of Irish royal blood in 521. From an early age it was decided that his destiny lay with the Church and he was educated at several religious schools, ending up as a pupil of the great Christian intellectual St Finnian at his monastery at Clonard. Here he passed his days studying and copying old manuscripts. Then at the age of twenty-five he decided upon a more practical contribution to the Celtic Church and began wandering across Ireland, founding churches and monasteries as he went. By the time he was forty he had established 37 religious houses in Ireland, and could no doubt have afforded to settle down and consider his life's work completed. However, fate intervened to force him into self-imposed exile. There are many legends as to what caused him to abandon Ireland. One version has it that he illegally copied a Bible manuscript and refused to hand it over to the king when requested to do so. His stubbornness sparked off a civil war from which his warrior family emerged victorious. Filled by remorse at the deaths he had caused, Columba set sail with his 12 disciples vowing that he would never see Ireland again.

They first arrived at Kintyre and Aronsay, but they could still see a thin line on the horizon that marked the Irish shoreline, and so they set sail again, arriving eventually on Iona. Climbing a hill that afforded panoramic views, Columba was delighted to find that no trace of his homeland was visible, and the little band of brothers realized that they could settle on the inhospitable island. Once settled, the Irish monks began taking their message far and wide and in so doing converted most of pagan Scotland and northern England to the Christian faith. As the base from which they launched this programme of mass conversion, Iona would blossom into one of the most sacred religious sites in Europe, and its fame as a centre of learning would spread throughout Christendom, turning it into an important place of pilgrimage for several centuries.

The remaining years of Columba's life after establishing his monastery on Iona were largely devoted to preaching to the inhabitants of northern Scotland. He performed many miracles, and also provided for the instruction of his converts by founding numerous churches and monasteries. By the summer of 597, Columba knew that his end was approaching, and on Saturday, 8th June, he ascended the hill that overlooked his monastery and blessed it for the last time. That afternoon he attended vespers, and later when the bell summoned the community to the midnight service he entered the church without assistance. No sooner had he

done so than he sank before the altar and there surrendered his soul to God, surrounded by his disciples. The monks buried him within the monastic enclosure and a century later his bones were disinterred and placed within a bejewelled shrine. When the Viking raids began it became apparent that Iona was a prime target, and so his relics were removed to Ireland and deposited in the church of Downpatrick, where history goes mute about them after the 12th century.

For several centuries Iona remained a place of learning and of pilgrimage. Forty-eight kings of Scotland, from Kenneth MacAlpin to MacBeth, were carried by boat on their final journey across the sound to Iona, onto the harbour and up the Street of the Dead (the medieval cobbled road, part of which is still visible outside the abbey church today) to the burial ground known as the Relig Oran.

Wealthy pilgrims brought money to the monastery, and this enabled the monks to set about creating some of the most exquisite artworks of the Dark Ages. Without doubt the finest of these is the elaborate *Book of Kells*, now displayed at Trinity College, Dublin. Iona's intricate Celtic high crosses are also impressive, such as the lovely 8th-century St Martin's Cross which stands before the abbey.

In 794 there occurred the first of the Viking raids that would eventually result in the decline of the monastery. In 806, 68 monks were slaughtered by the Vikings at Martyrs Bay, located just to the south of the modern-day ferry landing. The monastery was just too vulnerable and consequently by 825 it had been virtually abandoned.

The Island's fortunes were revived around 1200 when a massive building programme began and a Benedictine abbey replaced the old Columban monastery. An Augustinian nunnery, the ruins of which are passed on the way to the abbey buildings, was also established, and the island flourished again for several centuries, until the Scottish Reformation of 1560 ended its days of glory. The buildings fell into ruin and remained so until the early 20th century, when restoration work was begun. Finally, in 1938, a religious community was once more re-established.

Today, it is a truly special place to which pilgrims still flock from all over the world. It can be quite busy and in the summer months the hordes of tourists can be quite overwhelming. Fortunately, many of them are on a rather tight schedule and few venture beyond the well-trodden path from the landing stage to the abbey. Consequently, for those who stray into the island's secret glens and hollows, solitude can often be found, where the memories of pagan worship and Christian sanctity seem to blend effortlessly together. Indeed, it is in these places, surrounded by low-

OPPOSITE: *The grave of Robert Kirk in Aberfoyle's old Kirkyard gazes over the fields to Doon Hill, where the Reverend Kirk was said to have been abducted by the fairies.*

lying hills set against the backcloth of the shimmering turquoise waters of the Sound of Iona that you truly begin to get the measure of the place and find yourself agreeing wholeheartedly with Dr Johnson's astute assertion that the '...man is little to be envied...whose piety would not grow warmer among the ruins of Iona'.

THE FORT OF DUNADD
Nr. Kilmartin, Argyll
The Glen of Mysterious Ancient Monuments

Scattered across the landscape of Kilmartin Glen are more than 350 ancient monuments – 150 of which are prehistoric. They include burial cairns, rock carvings and standing stones, some of which date back 5,000 years, and all of which are fascinating to look at, giving as they do an opportunity to understand the customs and beliefs of the different peoples to whom this area has been home. One of the most significant and least visited of these relics is situated atop a rocky crag that rises 53m (175ft) above its surroundings, and from the summit of which are great views across a patchwork quilt of green fields, dark streams and gorse-covered hillocks. It is difficult to believe today, but between AD 500 and 900 this windswept and exposed rocky outcrop was one of the most important places in Scotland. The original Scots were migrants from Ireland who began settling in the region in ever-increasing numbers from 500 onwards. Here they founded their kingdom of Dalriada, of which Dunnadd was the capital – the place where their kings were anointed.

It was from here that they consolidated their grip on the land, ultimately absorbing their ancient neighbours the Picts, and by 843 Kenneth MacAlpin, King of the Scots of Dalriada, had also become King of the Picts. Unfortunately, the Viking raids of the 9th century necessitated the removal of the capital of the cojoined kingdom of Alba to Scone and Dunadd's days of glory drew to a close.

Today, little survives on the windswept outcrop to remember what an important place it once was. Yet to climb to its summit is a truly thrilling experience. It is reached by an exhausting, precarious and ankle-jarring climb, the latter stages of which involve scrambling over jagged-toothed chunks of bare rock. However, the struggle is more than worth it, for at the top you feel that you are standing on the bedrock of history, and the ages just seem to peel away. A partial section of the original wall from the fortress is still visible and on a rock slab, a little way beneath the summit, there is a carved bowl whose original purpose is unknown, but which may well have been used in the rituals surrounding the royal inauguration ceremonies. Nearby is

OPPOSITE: *Struggle up the slopes of the rocky crag on which the remnants of Dunadd Fort stand and you are walking amongst the ruins of the ancient Kingdom of Dalriada.*

some inscribed *ogam* text (an alphabet of straight lines), the meaning of which has never been deciphered, and a rough carving of a boar. The most intriguing carving is the imprint of a foot carved onto one of the rocks. It is believed that, following the Irish tradition, this is where the kings of Dalriada were inaugurated by placing a foot into the rocky indentation. By placing your own foot in the indentation you feel a real and mystical link that stretches back across the ages and brings to life the power and the history that surrounds you on this windswept summit where the Scottish nation was born.

ROSSLYN CHAPEL
Roslin, Midlothian
Menacing Gargoyles & Grimacing Grotesques

In 1446 Sir William St Clair, the third and last Prince of Orkney '...his age creeping on him, came to consider how he had spent his times past, and how he was to spend his remaining days. Therefore, to the end, that he might not seem altogether unthankful to God for the benefices he received from Him, it came into his mind to build a house for God's service, of most curious work...' He therefore set about the construction of what is probably the most enigmatic ecclesiastical foundation in the whole of Britain, a structure that he intended to call the Collegiate Church of St Matthew, but which is now known simply as the Roslyn Chapel. Sir William did not survive to see his dream reach fruition, for he died in 1484 and was buried in the unfinished chapel, and the larger building he had planned was never completed. What was built, however, is absolutely extraordinary. The internal decoration of the Roslyn Chapel is so detailed and intricate that it is often referred to as a 'tapestry in stone', and people flock from all over the world to gaze upon, ponder the meaning of and even decipher the incredible carvings that adorn its walls.

Menacing gargoyles and grimacing grotesques scowl down upon you as you approach the ornate, though decaying, stone doorway of the chapel. Inside, the barrel-vaulted roof is richly adorned with delicate carvings of daisies, lilies, roses and stars. An angelic orchestra is engraved about the walls, but so too are stone demons, saints, martyrs, lions and pagan green men, while ferocious dragons coil around intricately carved columns. Some of the engravings are even said to depict such exotic items as cactus and sweetcorn, which is a remarkable achievement considering that they predate Columbus's arrival in America in 1492. There are carvings that depict biblical scenes such as the fall of man, the expulsion from the Garden of Eden, the birth of Christ, as well as his crucifixion and subsequent resurrection. Many of the etchings are so complex and intricate that it has been claimed that the elaborate stonemasonry of the church is nothing less than a secret code which conceals the whereabouts of fabulous and mysterious treasures.

Without doubt the most involved of all the remarkable carvings are those that adorn the so-called Apprentice or Prentice Pillar, and the story behind its creation is both fascinating and tragic. The master mason was requested by the founder to carve this pillar exactly in the style of a specific one in Rome. Unwilling to commence work without first viewing the original, he set off for Rome to prepare for the task. While he was away his apprentice dreamt that he had finished the column and, with the details still fresh in his mind, set to work on carving the pillar himself. When the master returned he is said to have been so envious at the superior skill demonstrated by his pupil that he flew into a rage and struck the unfortunate boy across the head with a mallet, killing him instantly, a crime for which he was hanged. There is a theory that at the centre of the Apprentice Pillar is a lead casket in which is hidden the legendary cup used by Christ at the Last Supper and later used to collect his blood, the so-called Holy Grail. Such theorizing might be expected to draw dubious groans anywhere else, but there is something about the Rosslyn Chapel that truly does convince you that there is much more to this place than meets the eye, and that anything, no matter how unbelievable it might sound, could indeed be true.

DOON HILL
NR. ABERFOYLE, PERTHSHIRE
The Fairy Hill

In the quiet and peaceful disused kirkyard a little way past the bustling town of Aberfoyle, there stands the roofless shell of the old kirk to the rear of which you will find a tabletop tomb on which is etched the inscription: 'Robertus Kirk Aberfoile pastor 14th May 1692.' Robert Kirk was born a seventh son (said in Gaelic legend to be capable of second sight) in Aberfoyle. He began his career as Episcopal minister to the parish of Balquihidder, before returning to Aberfoyle, following the death of his father, to become the incumbent minister. Robert Kirk should be remembered as the first man to translate the Psalms into Gaelic. However, he also had an absorbing fascination with the enchanted world of fairies, and it is for another publication, *The Secret Common-Wealth of Elves, Fauns and Fairies* (1691; though not actually published until the 19th century) that he is best known today.

His book contained detailed descriptions of the society and customs of the fairy folk, and even went so far as to describe the food eaten by them. As such the locals came to believe that Kirk had committed a great transgression, that of giving away the closely guarded secrets of the fairies, and it was whispered in hushed tones that they would be certain to exact their revenge.

Across the fields from Robert Kirk's grave there looms the

tree-clad bulk of Doon Hill – the Fairy Hill as it is known locally. On 14th May 1692 Robert Kirk set off on his daily walk to the summit of this mysterious hill. He never returned alive and later his body was found on its slopes. He had, apparently, collapsed and died from a heart attack. Of course

ABOVE: *St Columba's cave is a dark yet sacred place where the saint who brought Christianity to Scotland once sought solace.*

rumour was rife that the fairies had been responsible for his fate, and it was widely believed that he had been taken by the fairies. According to the Reverend Patrick Graham, one of Kirk's successors in the 19th century, Kirk had actually appeared to one of his family after his funeral and told him how he had fallen into a swoon on the hill and had been spirited away to fairyland. He asked that a message be taken

to his cousin, Graham of Duchray, that his release could be obtained at the christening of his posthumous child. He promised that he would appear at the Baptism and that Duchray must throw a knife over his apparition to break the spell and release him from captivity. Unfortunately, when Kirk did duly appear at the ceremony, his cousin was so terrified that he was unable to take the required action and Robert Kirk's fate was sealed. It is said that he remains in the realm of the fairies to this day, where he acts as a mediator between their world and ours.

Having enjoyed the peaceful quiet where the mortal remains of Robert Kirk may, or may not, lie, a walk up the slopes of Doon Hill becomes an absolute necessity. It is a powerful and unusual place over which an eerie and enchanting silence seems to hang heavy. The trees that line the slopes lean at awkward angles and holly bushes abound. But strangest of all is that every spare branch and shrub has bits of torn cloth fluttering from them, each one inscribed with a wish or a message, many of them from children, asking for the fairies to intercede and assist with everything from stopping dad snoring to curing long-standing ailments. Also, small offerings of dolls and coins have been pushed into holes and it is easy to picture these as entrances into another domain, a magical kingdom from which the fairies might well troop out at night to grant these fluttering wishes that clothe the summit of Doon Hill in a veil of genuine mystery and enchantment.

ST COLUMBA'S CAVE
Nr. Ellary, Kintyre
The Man of God's Retreat
Tradition holds that this secluded and peaceful little cave was the place where St Columba carried on his ministry while petitioning King Conal for permission to establish his monastery on Iona in 563 (see page 149). The narrow, muddy track that leads to it is shaded by a dense covering of towering trees that cast it into perpetual twilight as it twists its way through thick bracken and clinging bramble. Suddenly, the cave appears before you, its entrance guarded by two huge slabs of moss-covered rock. Squeezing past them you find yourself in a dark little cavern where a soothing aura of deep spirituality soon overcomes you and you begin to fall under the spell of the serene simplicity of what is, without doubt, a holy and mystical place.

A small stone altar that sits to the right as you enter is said to have been Columba's holy shrine. Above it a crude cross carved into the wall has been outlined in thick white paint, giving it an eerie quality. On the opposite side from the

OPPOSITE: *Keills Chapel sits peacefully on a heather-carpeted hillside and contains the most remarkable collection of grave slabs and stone crosses imaginable.*

entrance a set of steps lead down into a smaller cave, which may well have been an inner sanctum for deeper contemplation. It makes a perfect retreat in which to focus your thoughts on all things mystical, while contemplating the life and times of a man of God whose shadow reaches out to us from Scotland's distant past, and whose influence is still as strong today as ever it was in his own time.

KEILLS CHAPEL
Nr. Keillmore, Kintyre
A Splendid Place of Worship
Standing alone on a heather-carpeted hillside and sandwiched between Loch Sween and the Sound of Jura, this squat grey building does not at first glance strike you as being particularly attractive or welcoming. Yet, on stepping through the modern north door, it comes as a complete surprise to find yourself gazing upon the most remarkable collection of grave slabs and stone crosses imaginable. Brought inside to protect them from the ceaseless onslaught of the elements, they have been carefully arranged around the chapel's edges and provide us with a tantalizing insight into the unshakable faith and cherished beliefs of long-ago worshippers.

Most of the grave slabs date from the 14th–16th centuries, while the older parts of the chapel probably go back to the 12th century. Illumination is now provided by modern roof lights, but it is still possible to gain an impression of how stirring and magical an experience it must have been when the lighting depended on the four windows that puncture the rough, stone walls – three of them concentrating their light onto the altar and its surrounding area.

The chief glory of this unexpected little building is without doubt the Keills High Cross, which for centuries stood outside to the north-west of the chapel but which, owing to the effects of weathering, has now been brought inside and its original position marked by a replica. This fine example of early Christian art probably dates from the 8th century. It is richly decorated and shows the dominance of the Irish influence in these western parts of Scotland. The cross centre is a boss (sometimes known as a bird's nest design), the shaft displays a chevron pattern and shows the faint figure of a praying monk above, interlaced animals are carved onto the side arms, while a winged angel-figure surrounded by Celtic interlacing adorns the top arm. The cross is beautifully framed by a tiny arched window through which moody, rolling hills can be glimpsed and the overall effect is awe-inspiring.

As you approach the chapel it looks so small and desolate that you imagine yourself spending no more than a few minutes here before moving on. However, once inside you find yourself captivated by the sheer magnificence of the simplicity that surrounds you, and those few minutes can easily stretch to an hour or more as you sit entranced by this glorious place of ancient worship.

Further Reading

Ashe, Geoffrey *Mythology Of The British Isles*, Methuen, 1990

Atkinson, Tom *The Empty Lands*, Luath Press, 1994

Atkinson, Tom *The Roads To The Isles*, Luath Press, 1994

Berthelot, Anne *King Arthur Chivalry and Legend*, Thames and Hudson, 1997

Bord, Janet and Colin *Mysterious Britain*, Thorsons, 1995

Byrne, Tom *Tales From The Past*, Iron Market Press, 1977

Chambers, Anne *Granuaile*, Wolfhound Press, 1998

Curan, Bob *The Creatures of Celtic Myth*, Cassell and Co, 2000

Dames, Michael *Mythic Ireland*, Thames and Hudson 1996

Dixon, Mike *Arthurian Myth and Legend*, Brockhampton Press, 1998

Folklore, Myths and Legends of Britain, Readers Digest Association Ltd, 1977

Gregory, Lady *Irish Mythology*, Chancellor Press, 2000

Home, Gordon *Medieval London*, Bracken Books, 1994

Holt, J. C. *Robin Hood*. Thames and Hudson, 1982

Jones, Richard *England's Favorite Cities*. Macmillan, 1994

Jones, Richard *Haunted Britain and Ireland*, New Holland, 2001

Jones, Richard *Memorable Walks in London*, 4th Edition Hungry Minds, 2001

Jones, Richard *That's Magic*, New Holland, 2001

Jones, Richard *Walking Haunted London*, New Holland, 1999

Jones, Richard *Myths and Legends of Britain and Ireland*, New Holland

Mason, John *Haunted Heritage*, Collins and Brown, 1999

McHardy, Stuart *Scotland: Myth, Legend and Folklore*, Luath Press, 1999

Neeson, Eoin *Celtic Myths and Legends*, Mercier Press, 1998

Randles, Jenny *Supernatural Pennines*, Robert Hale, 2002

Ross, Anne *Folklore of Wales*, Tempus Publishing, 2001

Scott, Reginald, *The Discoverie of Witchcraft*, Dover, 1972

Simpson, Jacqueline and Roud, Steve A *Dictionary of English Folklore*, Oxford University Press, 2000

Slavin, Micahel *The Book Of Tara*, Wolfhound Press, 1996

Swire, Otta F. *The Highlands and Their Legends*, Oliver and Boyd, 1963

Turner, Mark *Folklore and Mysteries of the Cotswolds*, Robert Hale, 1993

Wales, Tony *A Treasury of Sussex Folklore*, S B Publications, 2000

Westwood, Jennifer *Albion, A Guide To Legendary Britain*, Book Club Associates, 1986

Zaczek, Iain *The Book of Irish Legends*, Cico Books, 2001

Index

Acknowledgements

The research for this book has taken me all over Britain and Ireland and numerous people have generously contributed their time and ideas to the project. Staff at local libraries helped me locate the sites in their locale. People at castles, landmarks even local service stations were always there to proffer opinion and point me in the right direction. To others I was just a voice on the end of a telephone, trying to confirm dates and facts. To all of you I offer my sincere thanks.

At New Holland Publishers I would like to thank Charlotte Judet for her patience and assistance, Jo Hemmings for her encouragement and Gülen Shevki-Taylor, whose evocative design is always such a pleasure to see. I would like to thank John Mason for his many suggestions and magnificent photography. On a personal level I'd like to thank my sister Geraldine Hennigan for patiently listening and for making useful suggestions, and also my wife, Joanne, for being there when I needed to test different entries and without whose patient understanding I would have been lost. A big thank you also to my sons, Thomas and William, who showed admirable interest for a four- and a six-year-old as they plodded patiently around with me!